Conceived, researched, written, designed, and photographed by Paul Sahre with the assistance of Peter Ahlberg, Jake Gorst, Michael Northrup, William Morgan, Andrea Koch, Loren Flaherty, Jonathan Han, Ulrike Schwach, and Michiel Van Wijngaarden.

# *Leisurama Now* *

Cover—Leisurama circa 1968 and the Atlantic Ocean with apologies to Ken Josephson

* Since "Now" in the title is perhaps illusory and imprecise—for the purposes of this book—"Now" refers to the date this book was published.

FOR E.O.

# PREFACE

The Philadelphia Experiment, Cranberry Street,
and the Endless Summer

February in Montauk is not pretty. Situated at the easternmost tip of Long Island, it is gray, cold, windy, and mostly deserted during the winter months. Definitely not a place you can easily envision as a summer destination.

But nonetheless I found myself there, in the winter of 2001 with my friend Nicholas Blechman—a fellow graphic designer who lives in Brooklyn—and a real estate agent from Sea 'n' Sun Realty. We were hoping to find a modest beach house that we could rent for the upcoming summer.

Why Montauk? Since moving to New York in the fall of 1997, I had yet to venture out to "The End," despite my curiosity about the place. Not only was Montauk said to be a low-key alternative to the Hamptons (which we couldn't afford anyway), but interesting rumors and stories about the place abound (long before it was the backdrop for the film *Eternal Sunshine of the Spotless Mind*): alien abductions, nude beaches, surfing, time-travel experiments, unexploded ordnances, and biological testing. Much of this is rumored to have happened in and around Camp Hero, an off-limits cold war–era army base just east of the town.

We asked our real estate agent if she could show us the cheapest house she had, and did she have any information about time-travel experiments in Montauk? Seemingly ignoring both questions, she proceeded to show us a number of rental houses, none of which were in our price range. By late afternoon, with our prospects dwindling, we arrived at Cranberry Street in Culloden Shores, a small community of ranch-style houses just north of town on the bay side. As we pulled into the driveway, I remember being unimpressed but happy because it seemed like we had arrived at a rental we could afford. The house looked like a typical suburban ranch, very similar to one I grew up in in upstate New York. When we entered we found a surprisingly quirkey, well-designed '60s-era interior that looked more like a place you would come home to after a day on the slopes, not a day at the beach. It also seemed much larger on the inside than it looked from the outside. As Nicholas and I walked around, we started thinking we had found our beach house. It was at that point that the real estate agent said that this house was called "Leisurama," and the two of us looked at each other and in unison said, "we'll take it." (see Tour, pages 48–58)

Our decision to rent was later re-enforced when we learned that our beach house came with a logo (see page 23)—perfect for a couple of graphic designers—as did the precisely 164 other Leisuramas all around us in Culloden Shores: next-door, up and down the block. Leisuramas everywhere. These houses constituted a '60s high-design-meets-low-cost marketing scheme that offered the average American a well-designed and affordable second home. The house was originally displayed at Macy's Department Store and came with "everything": furniture, appliances, curtains, towels, etc., much of which was still in our Leisurama. We also learned that the Leisurama was designed by the famous industrial designer Raymond Loewy and that a Leisurama had been the site of the famous Kitchen Debate between Nixon and Khrushchev. Although both of these facts turned out to be technically untrue, at the time they added to the mystique of this odd little building we had decided to rent.

One of my favorite things to do that summer was to just walk around the neighborhood. The experience was not unlike watching a scene in Godfrey Reggio's film *Koyaanisqatsi* (only without the soundtrack); one could almost see the neighborhood morphing into something else in fast-forward. Since the buildings were originally identical, each alteration made over time (and sadly, each Leisurama that's torn down), is made visible, even if the motivation behind each change is not. Changing tastes? Necessity? Privacy? Or keeping up with and/or differentiating oneself from the Joneses? Every addition, add-on, shrub, and personal touch is magnified and has contributed to the neighborhood's present appearance, which, one can easily imagine, is very different than it was last week, last year, etc…and certainly different than originally planned in 1964. All of this change must have driven the architect nuts, I thought.

During my third summer renting on Cranberry Street (August 2003), I asked photographer Michael Northrup to come out to the beach to invoke Ed Ruscha. Over a three-day period we photographed—as unjudgmentally as we could—every Leisurama in Culloden Shores from the exact same perspective. This collection of "mug shots" was the first step in convincing a publisher that Leisurama would make an interesting book. I can envision a person at some point in the future wandering around Culloden Shores—book in hand—astonished by how much has changed since each picture was taken.

Although not my intent from the outset, perhaps this book provides an answer to the question that our real estate agent ignored. If you are interested in time-travel experiments in Montauk, don't waste your time looking for it at Camp Hero; just take a walk around Culloden Shores. —*PS*

# LEISURAMA:
# A BRIEF HISTORY

William Morgan

The housing development called Leisurama contributed one of the most intriguing chapters in the history of our country's love affair with modernity, vacations, and living easy. Leisurama was the embodiment of the post–World War II American dream—at least the part of the dream that envisioned a second home at the beach.

The Leisurama story is a remarkable one, and the history of these houses is still evolving, even though they were constructed in the early 1960s. Most of the Leisurama homes have been converted to year-round occupancy, and with very few exceptions all have been enlarged and redecorated, while the once-barren shore is now forested. In a sweet paradox, these originally very affordable homes were looked down upon by more well-to-do neighbors but are now desirable and expensive, even "collectible." On the highest level, Leisurama is an important chapter in American architecture and housing—a living experiment in how we live and play. But the people who chose to believe in the Leisurama concept in the 1960s altered it in subsequent decades as their needs and expectations changed.

How these affordable and uniquely marketed second homes wound up on a peninsula called Culloden Point in a subdivision named Culloden Shores in Montauk is a yarn in itself. It involved a cast of characters ranging from Vice President Richard Nixon to the world's most famous industrial designer, local real estate entrepreneurs, and salesmen on the ninth floor of

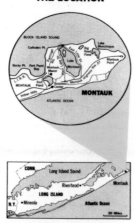

1.1

1.2

Fig. 1.1—Map detail from All-State Properties's sales materials

Fig. 1.2—*H.M.S. Culloden*

Macy's Department Store in Herald Square. It is the tale of a very special place, one that has a long and unusual history. It almost seems that the Leisurama project could not have happened anywhere else but Montauk, for it was largely the result of this unique place, which locals lovingly call "The End."

Looking at a map of the eastern tip of Long Island, where the sea-saturated land splits like a lobster claw, it is easy to understand how it was only a matter of time until the area would become the fashionable outpost of beautiful and wealthy New Yorkers it is today. While Montauk is politically part of the Town of East Hampton, it is culturally and physically a separate place. (Fig. 1.1) At the very narrow tip of the island, ten miles beyond the Hamptons, Montauk seems like another world. The land is flanked closely on both sides by the ocean and thus there is only one road that goes there; even in the best of times it is far away and not easy to reach.

For almost three hundred years Montauk was what people farther in on the island called "the end of the road." Suffolk County was known for its potato farms, but Montauk was too sandy, too windblown for agriculture, although fishermen have always called it home. And until the advent of railroads and highways, it was just too far away. Montauk's isolation and its natural beauty would eventually become attributes and attractions in the twentieth century, but for a long time it was simply the eastern extremity of New York State—132 miles east of New York City and essentially miles from nowhere.

Isolated though it may be, Montauk was also a very strategic location—a kind of Gibraltar, Finisterre, Land's End, an early warning watch spot for the entrance to Long Island Sound and the approaches to America's most important harbor. During the American Revolution, Montauk was an important linchpin in the British Admiralty's coastal blockade. Leisurama's Culloden Point is named for a British warship that foundered there in 1781. *H.M.S. Culloden*, a seventy-four-gun ship of the line, had sailed from the West Indies to intercept French ships on their way to Newport, and ran aground in a January storm. **(Fig. 1.2)** The *Culloden's* cannons were dumped into the sea and the ship was scuttled. The wreck of the three-masted warship can still be seen in the shallow waters off the point, and divers spot the occasional cannon.

Maybe a lighthouse would have saved the *Culloden* from a watery grave; the ship's demise reinforced the idea of the need for such a structure at the tip of Long Island. George Washington authorized New York's first lighthouse to be built at Montauk in 1792; the 110-foot sandstone lighthouse was completed four years later. Its light, visible for nineteen nautical miles, is both a romantic landmark and a constant reminder of the mystery and danger surrounding Montauk Point. **(Fig. 1.3)**

Montauk's guardsman role was no less important in World War II, when a coastal defense base called Camp Hero was located there. **(Fig. 1.4)** And later during the cold war, Air Force planes sallied forth from the camp to monitor Soviet submarines. Camp Hero is now a state park, although part of it is still closed to the public, fueling lingering mysteries and conspiracy theories about what goes on there.

One of the spookiest legends relates to the Philadelphia Experiment (code name: Project Invisibility). This was a program in which Navy scientists tried to make ships invisible using electro-magnetic waves; some believers

Fig. 1.3—The Montauk lighthouse
Fig. 1.4—Restricted area at Camp Hero

1.3

1.4

swear that the Navy was able to make a ship disappear and reappear. Rumors about secret government studies involving explorations of the fourth dimension, mind control, and time travel still flavor the supernatural air around the base—not to mention claims of alien sightings (one woman claimed to have been abducted and raped by a "Reptoid").

More plausible is the possibility that weapons were stored in the camp's purportedly vast underground caves and that live ammunition awaits the unwary fisherman or hiker. Concrete wartime bunkers were built to look like summer cottages, while the radar station was reputed to look like a fishing village from the air. This sense of weirdness is part of a delightful but somewhat wacky Montauk worldview—one that easily accommodated the offbeat Leisurama.

In 1882, long before the days of real Nazi U-boats and alleged alien invaders, McKim, Mead & White created seven houses at Montauk. These cozy, shingled cottages were typical of the town's early settlement. Writers, artists, and their like-minded friends came out for the scenery and the salubrious air, but most visitors came for the unparalleled fishing and hunting. Montauk was something of a sportsman's heaven, albeit a rustic and delightfully undiscovered one.

Building upon this sense of Montauk as a playground of the athletic rich, Carl Graham Fisher, the developer of Miami Beach, dreamed of making it the "Miami of the North." **(Fig. 1.5)** He wanted Montauk to become the summer vacation spot for the wealthy yachtsmen and polo players who elegantly wintered in what had once been mangrove swamps. In 1925 Fisher purchased ten thousand acres of the South Fork for the low price of two-and-a-half million dollars. There was not much in the way of infrastructure, so Fisher set about building it all: homes, hotels, churches, golf courses, boardwalks, and downtown Montauk itself. Fisher needed a safe harbor for his yacht club, so he connected Lake Montauk with the sea.

Carl Fisher was one of those classic self-made American entrepreneurs in the Horatio Alger mold. He sold bicycles and automobiles, developed the Indianapolis Motor Speedway, and made millions on the sealed beam Presto-O-Lite for cars; he also championed cross-continental roads like the Lincoln and Dixie highways. But the man who re-engineered the landscape of south Florida and eastern Long Island was eventually defeated by hurricanes and the stock market crash of 1929. Fisher's "Monte Carlo on the Atlantic" had, nevertheless, created some of Montauk's basic services and shaped its landscape, while forever linking the upper crust with the former fishing village. The rise and fall of Fisher's real estate empire only added to Montauk's romantic reputation.

Hotel and resorts aside, there was a slow but steady growth of domestic construction in Montauk by wealthy city dwellers. One such place was Eothen, a Cape Cod–style cottage designed by Princeton architect Rolf Bauhan in the early 1930s and built right at Montauk Point. As Montauk became an "in" destination, the house achieved fame as a rental property for the glitterati, including Jackie Kennedy Onassis and the Rolling Stones. Andy Warhol and Paul Morrissey bought Eothen in 1971 for $225,000, and its recent multi-million-dollar asking price demonstrates the staggering inflation of real estate values in Montauk since the debut of the $12,900 Leisurama model.

1.5          1.6

1.7

Fig. 1.5—Carl Graham Fisher          Fig. 1.7—Aerial view of Levittown, Pennsylvania,
Fig. 1.6—Herbert Sadkin               ca. 1959

Eothen was one of the few houses built at Montauk during the Depression. Only a generation later Americans had fought and won the greatest of all wars. In re-integrating the returning veterans, huge chunks of Long Island were developed in seemingly endless rows of quickly constructed look-alike Capes and ranch-style boxes. Levittown was, of course, the best known of these. (Fig. 1.7) But Levittown and its imitators built first homes, designed for people who either commuted to New York City or worked in the various new industries that sprang up on Long Island during the war. Vacationing Levittowners with teenaged children were now packing up their families and heading to the new motels near the beaches.

Herbert Sadkin, a Long Island–based developer and president of the some-what vaguely named All-State Properties, realized the post-war generation needed second homes. (Fig. 1.6) As Alastair Gordon, an architectural historian of eastern Long Island, wrote in an article on Leisurama for *House & Garden,* "Sadkin dreamed of making millions by building a Levittown for leisure, a Levittown with sand." Ambitious, creative marketers like Sadkin zeroed in on the fact that vacations were not just for the wealthy anymore. It wasn't only sociologists and market researchers who instinctively understood where Americans might next want to spend their time and money. What better place to ride out the Cuban Missile Crisis than your cottage far, far from the main urban targets?

Nikita Khrushchev, unintentionally, helped boost Sadkin's dream of making the vacation home available to the middle class. Sadkin had gone to Moscow as part of the United States Trade Fair (officially called the "American National Exhibition in Moscow") in the summer of 1959, where

Fig. 1.8—The Kitchen Debate, U.S. Vice President Richard Nixon, center, and Soviet Premier Nikita Khrushchev left center.

Standing to the right is Khrushchev's deputy, Leonid Brezhnev, and developer Herbert Sadkin is second from left.

1.10

1.9

Fig. 1.9—Raymond Loewy
Fig. 1.10—William Snaith

the famous Kitchen Debate (Fig. 1.8) took place, in Sadkin's model kitchen, as the Soviet leader and Vice President Nixon publicly argued over the merits of their respective society's priorities. Nixon allowed that certain Soviet rockets had better thrust, but, "What we want to do is make easier the lives of our housewives." Khrushchev refused to believe that Sadkin's kitchen was typical, plus, it did show how lazy Americans were ("Don't you have a machine that puts food into the mouth and pushes it down?" he chortled).

Sadkin had already figured out that the kitchen—more than anything else—sold a house, and that the typical All-American Kitchen was the heart of a home model (the progenitor of Leisurama). Sadkin's public relations man (and later Nixon speechwriter) William Safire smuggled pictures of the cold warriors' exchange out of Russia in his socks, and their publication put the kitchen on front pages everywhere. (Recalling the name of the first satellite launched by the Russians in 1956—and making reference to the national hysteria that event caused—Safire dubbed the house Splitnik, which was also a response to the fact that they widened the house's hallway for the large crowds who visited the house at the exhibition).

Sadkin's choice of the Raymond Loewy/William Snaith firm to design his dream scheme was as smart as his marketing techniques. (Fig. 1.9–10) Although avant-garde architects at the Ivy League schools tended to dismiss Loewy as a minor figure, he was the total designer that they could only dream of becoming—not to mention that he was fabulously successful and rich (Loewy's face adorned the cover of *Time* magazine, the apogee of fame in America). There was little in the designed world that Loewy and his associates had not shaped and made better. Loewy's stream-

1.11

lined moderne could be seen in locomotives for the Pennsylvania Railroad, Hupmobile and Studebaker cars, buses for Greyhound, all sorts of appliances for General Electric, jukeboxes, Coca-Cola dispensers, and some of the major logograms of our times, including those for Exxon, Shell, and Lucky Strike. The Loewy outfit designed interiors, department stores, houses, virtually everything in search of a combination of functionality and panache. And it was Raymond Loewy to whom Jackie Kennedy turned when she wanted the right artist to design a postage stamp to honor John Fitzgerald Kennedy.

So it was no surprise that Sadkin approached the Loewy firm to design Leisurama in 1963. At the time, the great designer was far more interested in automobiles, and dividing his time between Paris and Palm Springs, so it was Snaith who solidified the relationship with Sadkin. The project was unveiled weeks before President Kennedy was assassinated in Dallas. The success or failure of the housing project was not related to that historical event; rather its launch that year placed it squarely in the optimism and headiness of the Camelot presidency.

Loewy assigned Sadkin's scheme to the vice president of his Housing and Home division, Andrew Geller. **(Fig. 1.11)** The son of Russian immigrants and a graduate of Cooper Union, Geller had designed public structures for the firm, such as banks and department stores—he did dozens of Lord & Taylor stores, including the one at Garden City built in 1956, and he even created their logo. He also designed products for Loewy, such as the 1954 Anscoflex camera ("Ask to see this modern gray and silver beauty at the next convenient camera counter," commands the advertisement).

Fig. 1.11—Andrew Geller

Although he was a twenty-eight-year veteran of the Loewy office, Geller's reputation rests upon a series of Long Island beach houses that he designed outside of office hours. His structures were uncompromisingly modern and characterized by sharp angles and unusual geometries (Geller earned the sobriquet, "wild man with a T-square"). In his book *Weekend Utopia: Modern Living in the Hamptons*, Alastair Gordon argues that, unlike the designers of the hyped-up, over-priced status cottages and megahouses of recent memory, the modern architects working in eastern Long Island created a virtual laboratory of first-rate domestic design. Percival Goodman, Antonin Raymond, and William Muschenheim placed flat-roofed cubes on the dunes in the 1930s.

Following the war, Le Corbusier walked the beaches of Montauk, and second-generation modernists like Pierre Chareau, George Nelson, Carl Koch, Philip Johnson, and Peter Blake experimented with house designs based on the new ideas of leisure. Montauk and the Hamptons, however, are better known for the work of the 1960s and '70s by architects such as Charles Gwathmey, Richard Meier, and Norman Jaffe. So Andrew Geller's work is in the middle of these important camps, and his Irwin Hunt House on Fire Island of 1958 graced the back cover of *Weekend Utopia*. Gordon later devoted an entire book to Geller, appropriately called *Beach Houses*.

A Geller beach house was quirky, generally affordable, and light-hearted, depending heavily upon bold geometry, often placed at unusual angles. His early A-frames were followed by much more complicated and intriguing shapes, constructed of rather inexpensive materials and having a pop art sensibility long before post modernism was a twinkle in Robert

Venturi's eye. Geller gave his houses descriptive but also evocative names—Reclining Picasso, the Cat, the Milk Carton, Raspberry Baskets, and the Monopoly House; there is also the Lighthouse, the Gull, and a church called the Whale.

Geller was thinking along these lines when he proposed a variety of designs for the new leisure village. Some Leisurama prototypes featured his usual oblique angles, although they were not quite as off-the-wall as the Fire Island beach houses. They were, however, just as good as the other modernist homes in the dunes with their broad expanses of glass. Sadkin selected the design that was, according to Geller, closest to existing ranch houses. Perhaps it is not so surprising that the chosen model was the simplest—and the most economical. Even so, the Leisurama design was adventurous, even if it was not as unconventional as Geller had hoped. The plans were revolutionary in their openness—especially for such a large, commercial project—echoing the open plans of Frank Lloyd Wright's Usonian houses of the 1930s and 40s.

The exterior, with its wide, sheltering overhang and its not so uncoincidentally Japanese character and vernacular modularity, also evoked memories of Wright, as well as Carl Koch's popular Techbuilt House. The Leisurama facades were dictated by the plan and the lots were small—one-third of an acre (or 7,500 square feet). The houses themselves were built on concrete slabs measuring between 730 and 1,200 square feet with picture windows and carports, but no basements. Although the look of the houses said "summer," Geller included sufficient insulation and gas heating to make them livable in the off-season.

1.12

1.13

1.14

Fig. 1.12—Convertible, 1964  Fig. 1.14—Villa, 1964
Fig. 1.13—Expanded Convertible, 1964

The houses came in two basic models. The smaller version, the Convertible was basically a studio: 730 square feet of open plan with a sofa bed and a folddown "Phantom" or Murphy Bed. **(Fig. 1.12)** A folding mahogany screen allowed the owner to divide the "living room" from the "study." The larger model, the Expanded Convertible, was 950 square feet, supposedly capable of sleeping eight, and included two or more bathrooms. **(Fig. 1.13)** (Ooh, the luxury! The apartment back in Brooklyn only had one toilet.) There was also a slightly larger, 1,200-square-foot model, the Villa, that was originally planned as a rental suite, but this idea proved unpopular and only four were built. **(Fig. 1.14)** Small, perhaps, but the houses seemed to promise not only ease of living, but low maintenance. The redwood siding and the interior paneling—including Philippine mahogany for the folding screens—came with a lifetime guarantee from U.S. Plywood.

Who really cares that much about what the getaway house looks like when you are spending your time in the water and on the sand anyway? As a resident who came here with her parents as a child remembers, "Living in Leisurama wasn't about the house itself…it was about walking to the beach any time of day"; all the houses were only a block from the ocean. But even if the houses were not so thoughtfully designed (and infinitely expandable, as we'll see), it was a tremendous bargain. Incredibly, a Leisurama house was very affordable: $12,990 for the small one and only $3,000 more for the larger one. The Convertible could be gotten for $490 down and $73 a month with a 30-year, 5.25% F.H.A.-insured mortgage. The larger house required an $87.90 monthly payment after an initial outlay of $940.

A house this cheap and right along the shore at Montauk could hardly be believed. But it was even more of a bargain, for the greatest selling point of Leisurama besides the location was that the house came fully furnished. In a beyond-brilliant scheme, Sadkin teamed with Macy's Department Store to supply a complete world of vacation living without the buyer having to do anything but select a few colors. The houses came with everything: furniture, appliances, a forty-five-piece Melmac dinner service and plastic glasses, fifty pieces of stainless steel flatware, plus towels, napkins, placemats, beds, pillows, and sheets—light bulbs and toilet paper were about the only necessities not included. **(Figs. 1.15–21)** As the general sales manager for Leisurama Frank Tuma noted, "It was the ultimate turnkey operation—down to the color-coordinated toothbrushes in the bathroom. All you needed were your clothes and a six-pack." Or as an advertisement bragged, "Leisurama's unique feature is that a key plus groceries is all you need to start housekeeping."

Tuma recalls thinking that the whole scheme was a bit wacky, yet two hundred Leisurama homes were sold in only six weeks, and he contends that they could have easily sold four times that number. These sales, amazingly, were based on only a handful of models, introduced to prospective buyers at Macy's main store in Manhattan, **(Fig. 1.22)** another at Roosevelt Field, and three in the village of Montauk. Leisurama has been called the first large-scale "branded housing project" in America, and it clearly was, in the words of Geller's grandson Jake Gorst, "sold like soap…they made it appeal to people like orange juice." **(Fig. 1.23)**

The Leisurama story is rarely told without some tale of a woman going to Herald Square to buy a bra and coming home with a house instead.

1.15

1.16

1.17

1.18

1.19

1.20

1.21

Fig. 1.15—Dacron pillow

Fig. 1.16—Loewy-designed table lamp

Fig. 1.17—Plastic drinking glass

Fig. 1.18—Stainless service for eight

Fig. 1.19—Melmac dinner service for eight

Fig. 1.20—Side chair

Fig. 1.21—Bath towels

1.22

1.23

Fig. 1.22—Leisurama display model located on the ninth floor of Macy's Herald Square store.

Fig. 1.23—The Leisurama logotype

Two sisters, Agnes and Lenore Scalley, bought a house after only a half-hour tour of the model at Roosevelt Field (Lenore said she was hooked by the paneling that did not need painting). Reinforcing the belief that kitchens sell houses, the Macy's models featured General Electric "carefree custom kitchens" with an "automatic dishwasher" and "estate-sized range," as well as combination washer-dryers. Recitations of domestic resources such as "decorator designed, custom bathrooms by Briggs," "long wearing full beauty floor covering by Armstrong," and Loewy lamps exerted a strong pull. (Fig. 1.24)

Macy's ran appealing full-page advertisements in the newspapers listing all the furnishings—chairs, lamps, drapery, four Dacron pillows, and a seven-piece set of aluminum cookware. "For sale: A way of life. Where? At Macy's." (see page 236) When breathtakingly faced with a fully stocked, complete model, people found it hard to turn down. It was affordable and required nothing but a down payment. The total package was a knockout: there were fewer options to choose from than on a car of the time—the main choice was lot selection. Montauk seemed a long way to travel for a New Yorker, but a trip to the sandy site was usually enough to hook a buyer. Not all made the trip, however, for the Macy's model was quite seductive. Once the contract was signed, builder Charles Piser started construction; not long thereafter, Macy's dispatched a truck with the promised furnishings. The owner only had to wait three months and then move in. The price, the location, and the furnishings made an irresistible package.

How could a venture that included Raymond Loewy, Macy's, and the marketing genius of the man behind the All-American Kitchen fail?

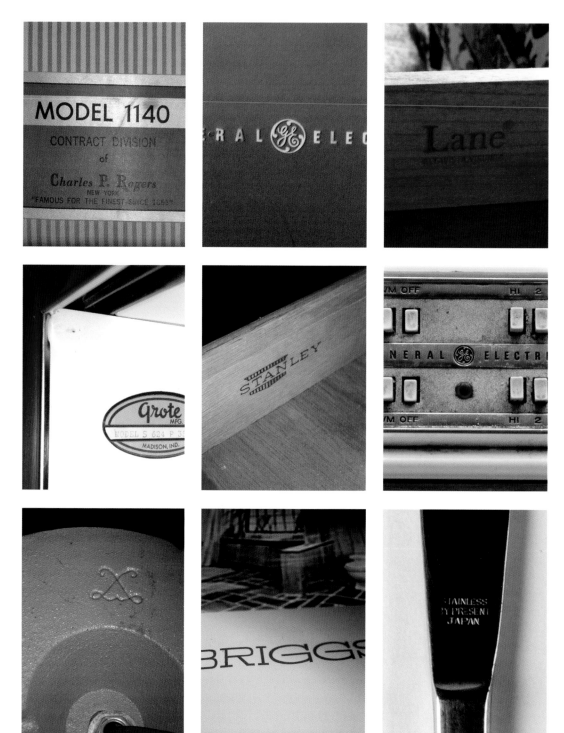

1.24

Fig. 1.24—A number of Leisurama's brand collaborators

38047
WEAR-EVER
ALUMINUM
TRADE MARK
MADE IN U.S.A.
7" DIA.

Monvent
ERS OF LEISU
OLD MONTAUK HI
MONTAUK POINT, L. I.,

MACY'S
OWN
BRAND
BEDDING

Stalwart

AL N0 4670
N0 1038

MACY'S OWN BRAND
Chatelaine
BY MARTEX
ALL COTTON EXCLUSIVE OF DECORATION

L-CO CABINET CO
SHOP ORDER        NAME
03661    LEISURA
F.P. BIRCH         HI
B-12

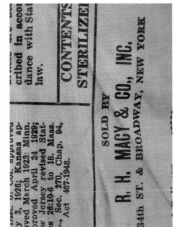

cribed in accor
dance with Stat
law.

CONTENTS
STERILIZE

SOLD BY
R. H. MACY & CO., INC,
34th ST. & BROADWAY, NEW YORK

y 3, 1926; Kansas ap-
yved March 1923: Minn.
proved April 24 1929;
w Jersey revised Stat-
s 26:10-6 to 18. Mass.
, Sec. 270, Chap. 94,
, Act 467-1948.

Sadkin planned one thousand Leisurama houses, but, the enterprise ground to a halt after the first two hundred were built because they simply were not profitable. Sadkin had understood the risks involved, but he decided to push forward despite warnings. Add to this the kind of unforeseen costs associated with any building project, a rise in land prices, and septic system problems, and any hopes of harvesting millions from the scrubby landscape of eastern Long Island were wiped out. (Sadkin did, however, build a Leisurama-like development near Fort Lauderdale in Florida; the house designs there were more conservative and the town, called Lauderhill, is now a small city of nearly sixty thousand people). So what seemed to be a model of adventurous architecture and housing was simply thwarted by the profit motive—bottom line trumped idealism. When All-State Properties went bankrupt, Macy's covered the project until the original houses were decorated and occupied.

Another sad bit of fallout from the demise of All-State Properties was the closing of the Leisurama exhibit at the 1964 New York World's Fair (see pages 218-221). Two Leisurama models—the Convertible that was built in Montauk, and a second model that was planned for Lauderhill, Florida—had been constructed at Flushing Meadows, sandwiched in a block among the Coca-Cola, DuPont, Seven-Up, and Dynamic Maturity pavilions (the models were converted to storage for Dynamic Maturity after the first summer). Still, the houses were seen by thousands of people, and they were popular. In some ways, the World's Fair was the apex of the Leisurama affordable vacation ideal. Like some of the fair's futuristic exhibits, Leisurama became like the memory of a promised piece of the future—a medical advance, a gadget that performed a task without human effort, a computer-driven car.

1.25

1.26

Fig. 1.25—Corner of Butternut and Cranberry streets, 1966.
Fig. 1.26—Corner of Butternut and Cranberry streets, 2007.

The affordable, well-designed, and fully furnished vacation paradigm was not achieved, but for those who had been so lucky as to buy one of the original Leisurama cottages by the sea, life was pretty good. Snootier Montauk neighbors (still holding onto Carl Fisher's polo-playing illusions of society grandeur, perhaps) had not been exceptionally welcoming to the upstart newcomers, referring to Leisurama as a slum. And, to be sure, the bulldozed sixty-five acres or so were pretty naked at first. Yet the scruffy coastal landscape came back with a vengeance, and coupled with landscaping efforts on the parts of owners, Culloden Shores began to look like other neighborhoods—more prosperous, less radical. (Figs. 1.25–26)

More than forty years on, nature has softened Leisurama's unpolished edges, while the owners themselves have made the most radical changes to the original design concepts. Many of the original vacationers decided to stay on in Montauk throughout the year, and the individualization of Leisurama happened almost immediately. Scholars have compared Leisurama to the Bauhaus, a kind of ultimate modernist design—the Arts & Crafts movement's *gesamtkunstwerk* espoused by Walter Gropius, the director of the influential German design school. At first, the spareness of Andrew Geller's designs suggested their modernist antecedents, but physical similarities aside, Montauk is not some northern European publicly supported housing—no Dutch social democratic village next to the sea. There were almost no options for the buyers, but Americans can be counted upon to individualize their homes upon moving in, and that happened at Leisurama. Just as there are almost no pure, unaltered houses in much the larger Levittown, only a handful of Leisurama houses are anything close to original.

Architect Geller's design was essentially no longer his when it left his drawing board at Raymond Loewy's. In fact, while Geller decried what he called insensitive box additions, he had never been crazy about the design of Leisurama—he loved the project because of the marketing. His ideal vacation home was light and airy; Leisurama, on the other hand, was soon transformed into a village of year-round homes. New paint changed the trim colors, the siding was replaced, and carports were converted into dens and bedrooms in the search for extra space. Some houses went upwards as owners added second stories; others were torn down and replaced with "newer style" homes. Patios, decks, and skylights further changed the basic cottages; new window treatments (the original wooden window frames did not fare well next to the sea), lanterns, balustrades, and decorative touches appeared. And how could they not? The houses may have been mass-produced, but there was no more chance of maintaining the original look than forbidding two hundred car owners to add bumper stickers, install white wall tires, or mount bobble heads on their dashboards. And if wives decided they didn't like green or blue Melmac dinnerware, what was to keep them from replacing it with new dishes, maybe even from Macy's? Besides the washer-dryer combinations never worked that well anyway, and the so-called Phantom Bed was best suited to farcical skits.

Admittedly, it would be wonderful to have an original and perfect Leisurama house as a museum to show how it was meant to be—an exhibit complete with all the original furnishings, 1960s lamps and chairs, and Macy's color schemes. But Leisurama has become something else beyond a historical artifact. It is, rather, a community that has evolved, and even if we wish for a pure version, we have to welcome what it has become on its own terms. We Americans are uncomfortable with ideology (and with most forms of modernism, when it comes to our houses), not to mention our discomfort with the architectural avant-garde. Part of being an architect means facing disappointment when your designs evolve or are altered, but even Geller has begrudgingly accepted that the community has changed over time. "It is as it should be," he has said.

So, how should we regard Leisurama now? Is it really about architectural idealism, well designed housing for the masses? Is it a symbol of American entrepreneurship and capitalism in the face of communism an Soviet militarism? Is Leisurama about branding, creative marketing and ambition? Or maybe it is a failure of capitalism, a casualty of Sammy Glick's scramble for money above all else? Utopian? Crassly commercial? Revolutionary? About individualism or conformity? Or is Leisurama just about average people wanting a place at the beach and the players willing to make that happen?

Leisurama, a living organism that is more satisfying for having broken the rules, can best be seen in the context of its location. Montauk is different: there is something about being at the end of the road, the end of the land, the end of the earth that imbues this place with an adventurousness, quirkiness, and sense of escape. Leisurama is one of Montauk's proudest legacies.

THE

PLACE

IS

MONTAUK

Notes

The following photographs were taken in the winter of 2007 in our (rented) Expanded Convertible Leisurama on Cranberry Street.

As I mentioned in the preface, the interior of this particular house has not changed much over the last forty years. Much of the original structure remains, as does a fair amount of the original furnishings and furniture.

A floorplan has been included at the beginning of each series of images with the camera position indicated by a colored dot.

A few changes of note:

Today, the walls are much darker throughout the house than they were originally. The mahogany paneling was stained a darker shade at some point in the past.

Leisuramas did not come with wall-to-wall carpeting. The floors would have been covered with a speckled tan vinyl tile.

The original fireplace was made entirely of brick. The wood burning stove has been added.

The original kitchen appliances have been replaced.

And in general, anything that is not in the inventory (see pages 59–86) should also be looked at with suspicion.

Compare these images with the two original interior renderings, which the prospective buyer would have seen in 1964 . (see page 235)

Whatever one might feel about forty years without a coat of paint, the interiors represented in this chapter are a close approximation of what I saw—as a prospective renter—when I first entered the house in 2001. Then consider that the amount paid to rent this house for three months in 2001 was the very same amount that it took to buy the house in 1964. —PS

48
49

Entrance area

FRONT

Entrance area (continued)

50
51

Entrance area (continued)

Livingroom/study

FRONT

Livingroom/study (continued)

Bathroom

FRONT

Kitchen/bedrooms

FRONT

Bedrooms (continued)

Bedrooms (continued)

# 4.

# INVENTORY

Furniture, Built-in Equipment, Appliances,
and Furnishings

(SCHEDULE A)

## INVENTORY NOTES

Cataloging an inventory of original furnishings for Leisurama was a confusing and time-consuming endeavor. This process, which I undertook with designer Peter Ahlberg, started almost immediately after I decided to begin work on this book in 2004 and continued up to the day files were handed off to my publisher in the fall of 2007.

While the relative worth of spending a decent part of three years visually documenting such items is perhaps dubious at best, we sure had fun doing it.

To build this inventory we had to rely heavily on a checklist originally supplied to each new owner by the Montauk Beach Company (see page 238). In the absence of any other concrete records about what Macy's, G.E., Briggs, Armstrong, et al. shipped out to Montauk in 1964–65, we started by supplementing this checklist with a verification method of our own.

To satisfy ourselves that an item was "in," we cross-referenced the inventory list with any photographs or artist's renderings that we came across. Some of these images accompanied the Leisurama sales material, but for the most part, we relied on period photographs in this process of which the photograph of the Moscow Kitchen Debate is an excellent example.

Note the G.E. combination washer–dryer to the right of Soviet Second Secretary Leonid Brezhnev (Fig. 4.1).

If no visual record of an item was available (which was the case with the majority of the items), we then put each item through a process: upon visual inspection, an item needed to look at least forty years

Fig. 4.1—Brezhnev and the Leisurama G.E. washer–dryer combination at the Moscow Kitchen Debate

old; if we found such an item in two or more houses or received verbal verification from two or more owners, we included that item. Overall the process was effective, but it did not always make for a definitive yes or no. The passage of time and fading memories made this process difficult; it also made it clear that there was not absolute consistency in the items that were included with each house. An example of this was a discrepancy in the Leisurama flatware design (Fig. 4.2).

Fig. 4.2—Both of these flatware patterns are original.

In the end, this process disintegrated into a desperate, beat-the-clock, door-to-door search with camera in hand. Ultimately, we found a surprising amount of original furnishings, although we were frustrated in our attempt to find and verify every item.

Once we decided that an item was original, we then used the inventory checklist to group all of these items into four categories: Furnishings, Built-in Equipment, Furniture, and Appliances. The category for each item is indicated by a different background color on the pages that follow (Fig. 4.3).

## INVENTORY CATEGORY

| Furniture | Furnishings | Built-in equipment | Appliances |
| --- | --- | --- | --- |

Fig. 4.3—The category for each item in this inventory is indicated by one of these colors.

After knocking on doors for three years—asking bewildered homeowners if they had a forty-year-old toothbrush or bath mat in the house—it is interesting to note the effect that hours of searching have had in distorting the value of some of the most insignificant items. A used, 39-cent toothbrush has become a kind of Holy Grail to us. This is how I feel about the items we could not find in time to be included in this book. While I am pleased that we were able to visually document most of the original items that were included with Leisurama, I am still losing some sleep over the items we couldn't find. —PS

2

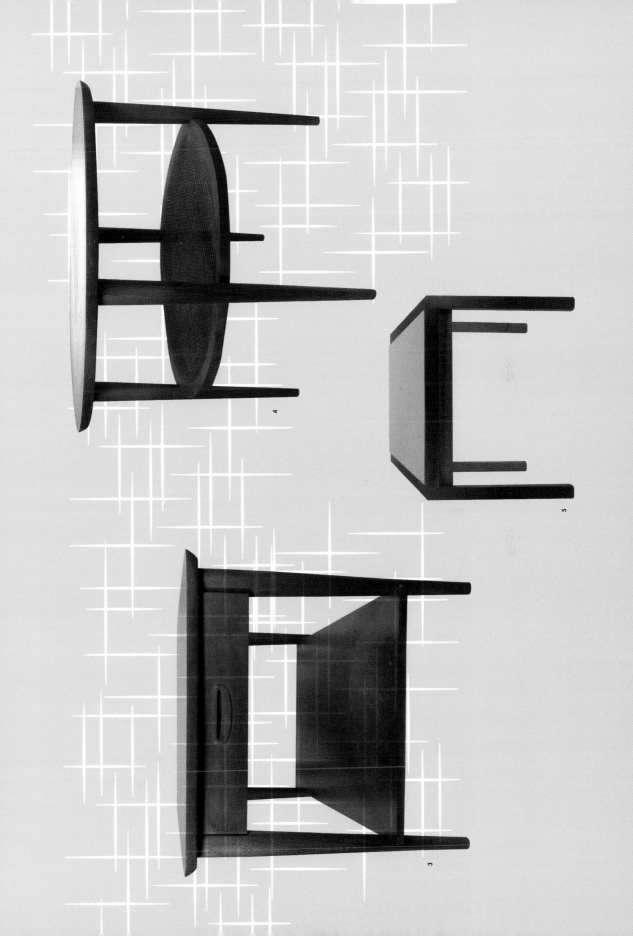

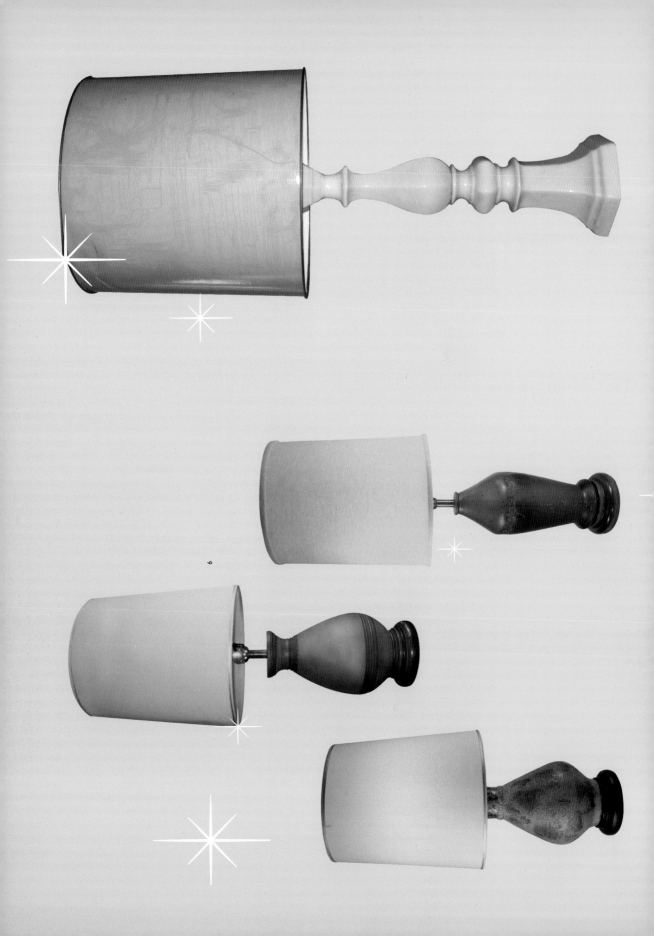

8

9

10

11

12

13

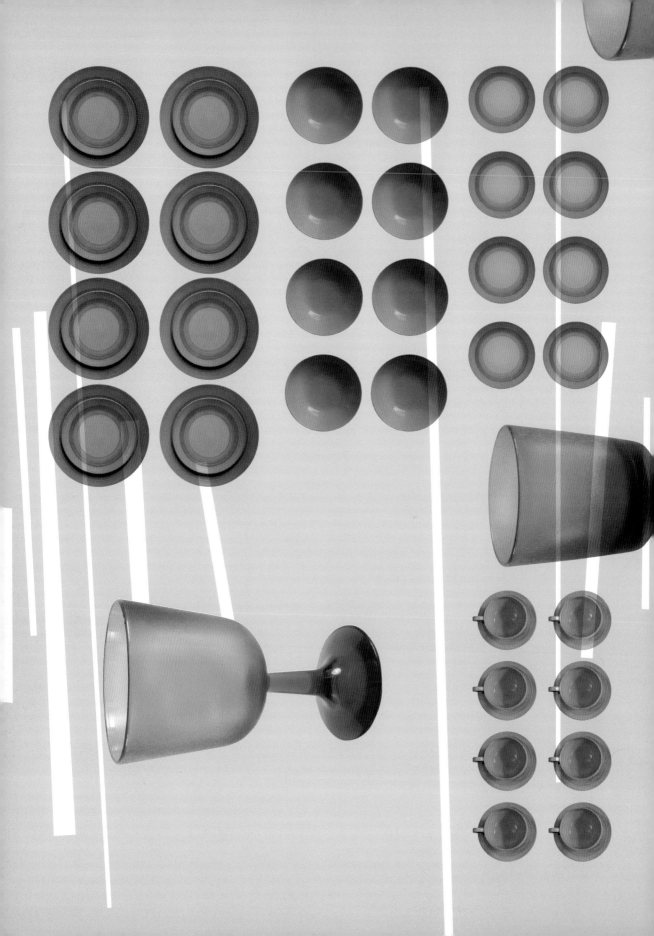

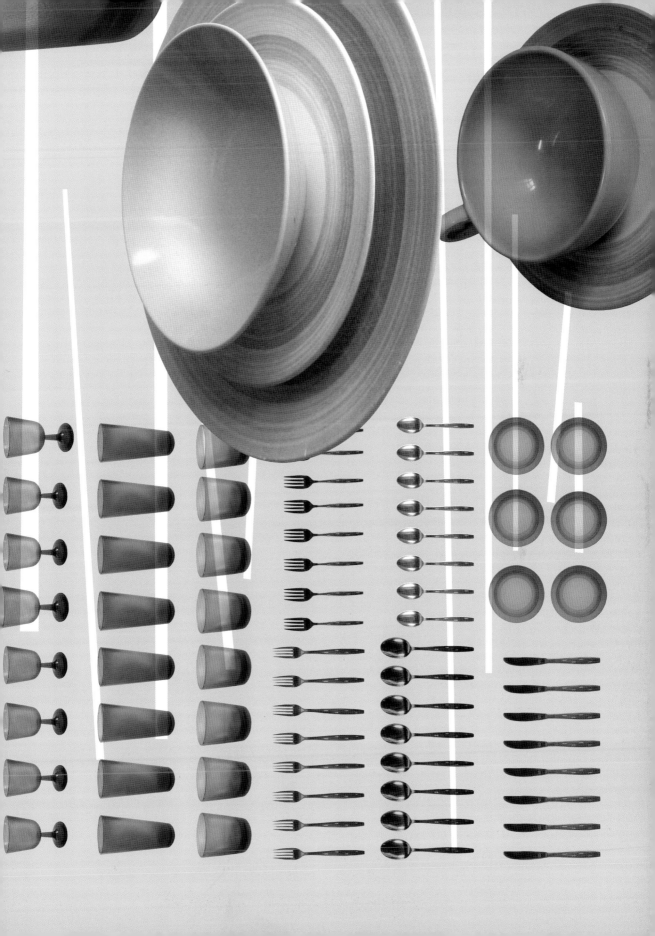

19

18

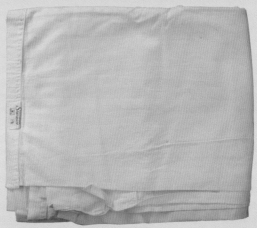

17

23

22

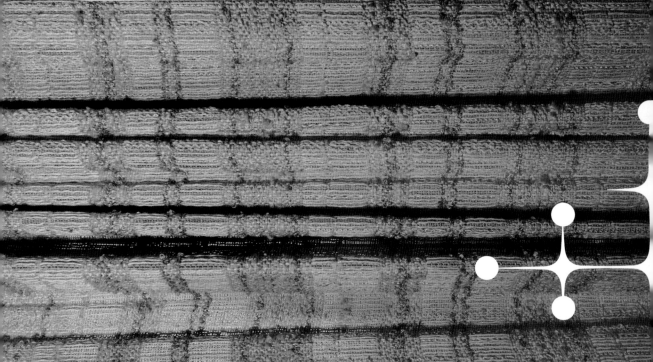

30

31

35

34

33

32

36

37

38

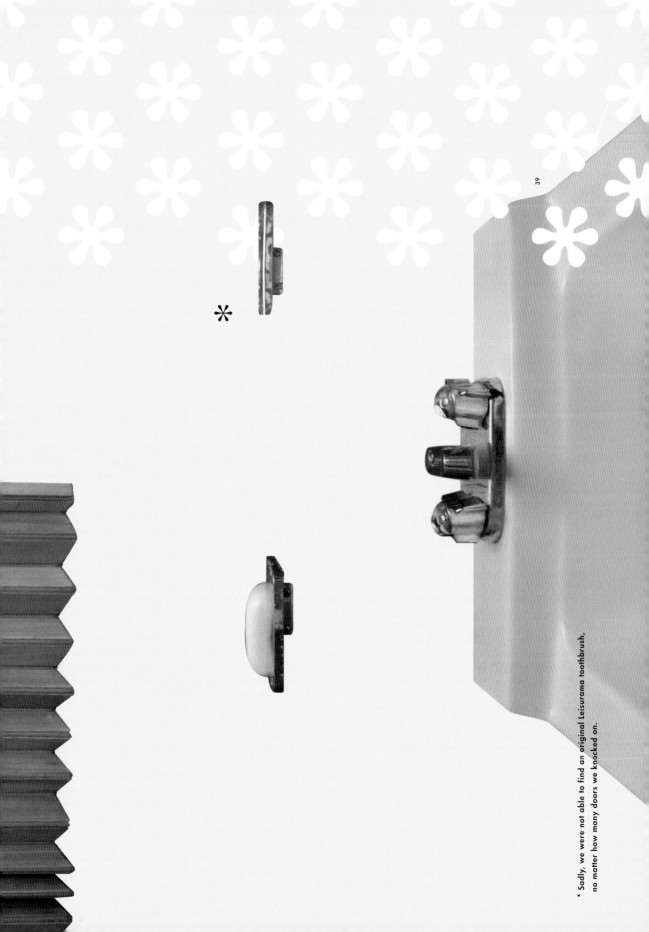

* Sadly, we were not able to find an original Leisurama toothbrush, no matter how many doors we knocked on.

42

43

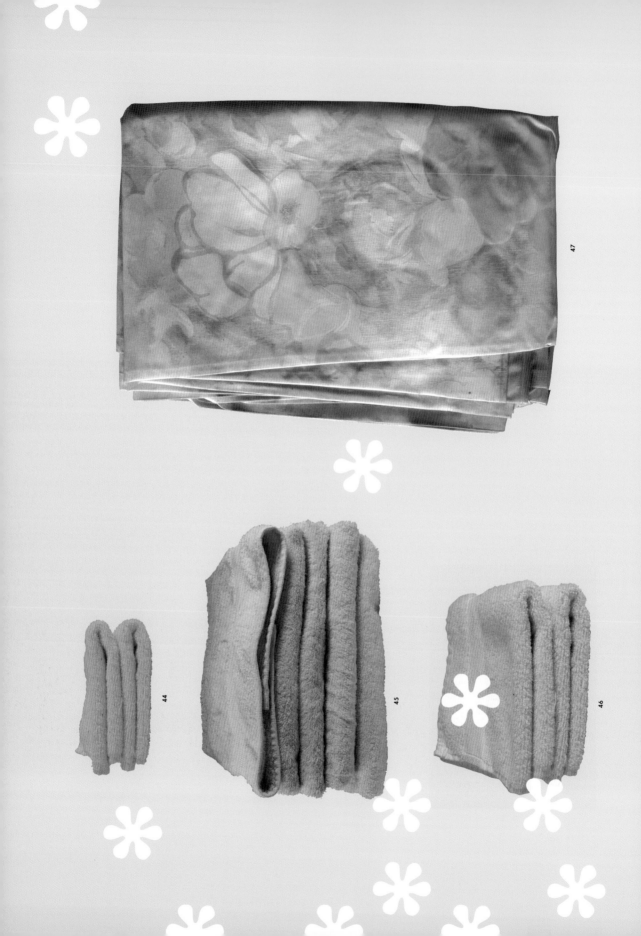

44

45

46

47

48

## NOTES (continued)

"All items have been tested by the store's bureau of standards...the decor is contemporary. Each item was chosen for attractiveness and quality as well as practicality." —*Leisurama sales brochure*

The furnishings on the preceeding pages were selected by Matthew Sergio, of the American Institute of Interior Designers, who was then head of Macy's decorating department.

### KEY

Each entry that follows includes the quantity of item, model (*C-Convertible, XC-Expanded Convertible*), and options if any. These appear at the end of each entry and are set in *italic*.

### 1. Side Chairs

This chair was, and still is, the most ubiquitous of all of the furnishings that originally came with the Leisurama. By my calculations, Macy's shipped at least 1,250 of these chairs out to Montauk in 1964–65, and many of these wood-and-woven cane chairs have managed to last somehow. The design feels more nineteenth century than mid-twentieth, which may be the reason they have stood the test of time with Leisurama owners. The Expanded Convertible came outfitted with seven of these chairs, which meant that they were—and still are—everywhere. *5/7, C and XC*

### 2. Drop-leaf Dining Table

This table converted from a long, narrow occasional table into a large dining table capable of seating eight. Four caster wheels allowed for ease of movement, and both sides could be raised and fixed in position, which would triple the surface area of this table when company arrived. This was a very handy item for a small vacation home, which accounts for the fact that this piece of furniture is still being used by a majority of the owners. *1, C and XC*

### 3. Rectangular End Table

Manufactured by Lane and inspired by mid-century Danish modern design, which was at the height of popularity in America in the early 1960s. Lane used mass-produced materials like wood-grained Formica to provide the look of the real article, but at an affordable price (see Round End Table) *1, C and XC*

### 4. Round End Table

This mid-century Scandinavian knock-off had a wicker shelf (see Rectangular End Table). *1, C and XC*

### 14. Stainless Flatware Service for Eight

We found two different patterns of flatware, each by Present, Japan. These designs can still be found in many kitchen drawers in Culloden Shores, mixed with newer flatware. *50 pcs., C and XC*

### 15. Plastic Place Mats

It's a miracle that we found a set of these. These are cheap laminated place mats one would have found in any diner of the period. *Color choice*

### 16. Set of Plastic Glasses

These translucent glasses—like the Melmac service they accompanied—were light, versatile, and fun, great for kids and easily taken to the beach for a picnic. *24 pcs., color choice*

### 17. Sheets

Stalwart, Macy's own brand. *8/16, C and XC*

### 18. Summer Blanket

There was no tag on the blanket we found. *2/4, C and XC, color choice, double*

### 19. Dinette Tablecloth

This item was not included in the "official" Leisurama checklist, but it cleared our varification process. The one we found was a bright blue vinyl with a linen texture and a white felt backing. It looks like it was never used and seems to be in its original plastic wrapping. Therefore: in. *1, C and XC*

### 20. Dinette Set

Metal tube construction with a padded vinyl seat. These were very easy to find, although most existing dinette chairs have been painted and have had their seats recovered. The tabletop is white and the metal base matched the color of the chairs. *1 table, 4 chairs, C and XC*

### 21. Dinette lamp (Electrical Ceiling Fixtures)

This lamp was installed in the area just off the kitchen above the dinette set: modern, clean, and very '60s. Today, these lamps are easy to find although I noted many instances where owners shortened the length at which these lamps hung. *1, C and XC*

### 22. Drapery

Original Leisurama curtains are a rare item in Culloden Shores. They can be found but are usually a sign of an original owner who is unwilling to part with them, even if they are showing signs of wear. Although the Leisurama sales material indicates that there were 30 fabric choices for draperies, we found only one—in various colors—that were designed to let in light even when drawn: perfect for a beach house. *3 sets/7 sets, fabric, and color choice*

## 5. Small Cocktail Table

Just the idea of a small cocktail table in one's home conjures up romantic images of '60s leisure living, but in reality these tables were used for much less fanciful purposes. Two such uses—as reported by Leisurama owners—were as a footrest and for eating in front of the television. *1, C and XC*

## 6. Lamps

The Macy's decorator must have been working under tremendous budgetery constraints in deciding which items to include. One can see this in the decision to include these lamps. They do not seem as considered as many of the other interior design decisions.
*3/8, C and XC*

## 7. Club Chairs

Each Leisurama came with two of these upholstered chairs. According to the artist's renderings in the Leisurama sales materials (see page 58), these chairs were meant to sit side by side in the living room. We found and documented two original fabrics—a bright green and a floral pattern (pictured)—although there may have been more offered. *2, C and XC, fabric and color choices*

## 8. Double Dressers' and Mirrors

Manufactured by Stanley to match the nighttables and headboard. Very minimal drawer pulls were the dressers' most distinguishing feature. *2, XC only*

## 9. Dacron Pillows

Dacron is a trademark for a durable polyester fiber that is used to make everything from pillows to men's suits to high-pressure fire hoses. *4/8, C and XC*

## 10. Nighttables

Manufactured by Stanley to match the dressers and mirrors. *3, XC only*

## 11. Double Headboards

Danish modern–influenced headboards for the bedrooms of the Expanded Convertible model. These pieces, along with the dresser and nighttables, satisfied the very American desire for matching pieces of furniture. *2, XC only*

## 12. Bedspreads

Colorful crosshatch pattern that brought the selected color theme into the bedrooms. *XC only, color choice*

## 13. Melmac Dinner Service for Eight

Melmac was a brand name for Melamine—a plastic that was popular in the '50s and '60s made by the American Cyanamid Company. Melmac dishware was affordable, light, tough, and versatile. *1, C and XC, color choice*

## 23. Set of Aluminum Cookware

Manufactured by Wear-Ever. Nearly every owner I spoke with dismissed this cookware, indicating that they replaced it almost immediately after moving in in 1965. Because of this, and the change in public opinion about the safety of aluminum in the years since, these items are scarce. *7 pcs, C and XC*

## 24. Built-in Kitchen Lighting (Electrical Ceiling Fixtures)

The kitchen and main bathroom featured drop-ceiling fluorescent lighting.

## 25. Kitchen Cabinets

These cabinets did not come with pulls; they were designed to be opened by pulling the beveled edges of each door or drawer. Few still exist in original condition. Many have been painted, and I found that a number of owners have added pulls.

## 26. G.E. Electric Range and Oven

Electric range with no-drip top, fast-heating Calrod surface units, with five different temperature settings at the push of a button. *1, C and XC, color choice*

## 27. G.E. Refrigerator

Single-door, left-to-right-opening General Electric refrigerator. It was almost impossible to find one of these still in use. Too bad—this one is so much cooler than most new fridges you can buy today, sorry. *1, C and XC, color choice*

## 28. G.E. Combination Washer-Dryer

Many report that this unique washer-dryer combination never worked very well. Perhaps this is what Vice President Nixon is discussing with Khrushchev during the Kitchen Debate (see pages 16–17). *Color choice*

## 29. G.E. Automatic Dishwasher

Many of these dishwashers are still in use today. From the manual for this appliance under "Dishwashing Hints": "Plate Warmer: To use your dishwasher as a plate warmer, rotate control dial clockwise to 'Dry' position, then latch door. Leave dishes warm for about 15 minutes." *1, C and XC, color choice*

## 30. Rug, 6' x 9'

This was a very ordinary shag rug that was designed for use in the living room. A number of owners remember replacing them for aesthetic reasons very early on. Others had no recollection whatsoever of this rug. *1, C and XC, color choice*

## 31. Floor tile

Every square foot of the Leisurama was covered by this brown speckled vinyl tile by Armstrong.

# NOTES (continued)

## 32–34. Electrical Ceiling Fixtures

Standard light fixtures one might find outfitting any suburban house of the period; 32 was located above the front door and 33 was also located outside, to the left of the side door; and 34 illuminated the small hallway between the two bedrooms of the Expanded Convertible model.

## 35. Built-in Phantom Bed

While researching each of the items in this inventory, I was surprised to find that many of the companies that collaborated on Leisurama are still in business. This is the case with Charles P. Rogers, whose contract division made this unusual bed. In this case, I was also surprised to find that they are located right around the corner from my office on Fourteenth Street in Manhattan. I walked over there to see if they could provide more information, and I was *not* surprised that they couldn't. *1, C and XC*

## 36. Accordion Room Divider

Many owners I spoke with were quick to point out this feature of their house. This item seems to be one of the most appreciated of the original furnishings, which accounts for the remarkably good condition of the screens that remain. Good thing—I can't imagine how one would repair one of these today. *1, C and XC*

## 37. Lightolier Lamp (Loewy Lamp?)

According to the Leisurama sales materials there was a Loewy designed lamp included with each house. I was able to determine that this beautiful lamp was manufactured by Lightolier, but I was not able to determine the designer. *1, C and XC*

## 38. Built-in Dressing Table

This item was built-in to fit between the closet and accordion room divider and located at the foot of the Phantom bed. This is a non-descript piece of furniture that seems out of place with the rest of the furnishings. *1, C and XC*

## 39. Bathroom Sink and Faucet (Plumbing Fixtures)

Beautyware bathroom fixtures by Briggs. Pictured is the sink in the 1/2 bath of the Expanded Convertible. *1, XC, color choice*

## 40. G.E. Heating Unit

The furnace in a beach house wouldn't get much use even after forty years. It has been suggested that the only reason that a furnace was included at all was so that Leisurama would qualify for F.H.A. financing. The houses were very lightly insulated, so those who passed on the fireplace when selecting their options and expected to be out in Montauk year round were in a world of hurt by mid-February. *1, C and XC*

## 41. Thermostat (Heating Plants and Fixtures)

The round Mechanical T87F Honeywell Thermostat has been an industry standard for over 40 years. It's modern look made it feel like home in 1964 just as it does today.

## 42. Bathroom Exhaust Fan (Heating Plants and Fixtures)

The original maufacturer of this bathroom fan, Emerson Pryne, does not make replacement parts for this unit anymore. They suggest that "It is often easier and less expensive to replace the entire exhaust unit through your local home center." And so another wonderful Leisurama detail bites the dust. *1, C and XC*

## 43. Heating Vent (Heating Plants and Fixtures)

Standard floor heat vent.

## 44–46. Bath Towels, Hand Towels, Wash Clothes

Chatelaine by Martex, Macy's own brand. I did find some of these items, but in each case they had long been relegated to secondary duty and could be found out in the shed, not in the bathroom closet. *4/8 of each, C and XC, color choice*

## 47. Shower Curtain

We found one of these but could not find an original bath mat. Probably lucky for us. *1, C and XC, color choice*

## 48. Toilet (Plumbing Fixtures)

Beautyware bathroom fixtures by Briggs. What summer house is complete without at least one of these? *1/2, C and XC, color choice*

# Leisurama Now

The Leisuramas of Culloden Shores
(As of September 2007)

○ EXPANDED CONVERTIBLE
● CONVERTIBLE
◐ VILLA (RENTAL SUITE)

XC

XC

XC

XC

C

XC

C

XC

C

XC

XC

C

C

XC

6.

# ANDREW GELLER'S
# LITTLE BOXES

Jake Gorst

The song "Little Boxes" was penned by Malvina Reynolds,[†] published in 1962, and made popular that same year by folk artist Pete Seeger. It was thought to have been inspired by the sea of tract homes in Daly City, California, however the lyrics resonated with non-conformists across the United States. To New Yorkers the song called to mind the sprawling suburbia of Long Island— the aerial imagery of William Levitt's Chiclet-like homes dotting curvilinear streets on the cover of *Time* magazine.

"Little Boxes" was the first song that fourteen-year-old Jamie Geller learned to play on the guitar. The song was a favorite of her family. By 1963, Jamie's father, Andrew Michael Geller, had become a well-known architectural designer. **(Fig. 6.1)** His freelance beach house work was featured in the *New York Times* and *Esquire* and *Life* magazines. Geller had just been appointed a vice president in the New York office of Raymond Loewy, the world-renowned industrial designer, and he would oversee the Housing and Home Products division for the next twelve years.

Geller's design philosophy was simple. "I wanted to give people elbow room and feel free," he said years later. "Free" meant breaking away from convention. The modern residential architecture of the 1950s and early '60s was predominantly characterized by post-and-beam construction. Many typical family homes were elongated, boxy forms with large floor-to-ceiling panes of glass. Geller was on a mission to skew the notion that modernism had to fit that mold.

[†] *Little boxes on the hillside/Little boxes made of ticky-tacky,*
*Little boxes on the hillside/Little boxes, all the same.*
*There's a green one, and a pink one/And a blue one, and a yellow one,*
*And they're all made out of ticky-tacky/And they all look just the same.*

Fig. 6.1—Andrew Geller, 1965

6.2

6.3

6.4

Early Geller beach houses were a variation on the rectangular box. The Irwin Hunt House, located in Ocean Bay Park, Fire Island, was a rectangular form rotated on axis. Bunkrooms were placed on opposite ends of the form. A cutaway view of the western bunkroom published in *Life* magazine resembled the 1921 painting *Lozenge Composition with Yellow, Black, Blue, Red, and Gray* by Piet Mondrian. The Pearlroth House, constructed in Westhampton Beach, consisted of two rectangular forms placed side by side and rotated on axis as well, earning it nicknames such as "The Double Diamond" or "The Box Kite." **(Fig. 6.3)**

By 1962 Geller began to produce exacto-style fenestration. One could imagine Geller using a larger-than-life razor blade to cut slits down the side of a structure, then prying back the studded walls and capping the resulting chasms with glass. As he later explained, "the age old technique of installing a flat rectangular shaped window in a building only allowed for the inhabitant to look straight out—or straight in. With my windows you could look in all directions—left, right, up or down."

Despite the fact that Geller's unique architectural style was gaining international attention, he recognized his primary responsibility as the breadwinner of the family. Art did not always pay the bills. While his freelance work provided a creative outlet for him, he continued to make the daily commute to Loewy's Park Avenue office. "The work was interesting to me," he said. "I enjoyed it. I always met new and interesting people." One such person was Herbert Sadkin, a Long Island property developer and owner of All-State Properties. Sadkin had been invited by the U.S. State Department to display a "typical American home" at the American National Exhibition

in Moscow. He was considering using plans for a ranch-style home drafted by Long Island architect Stanley Klein, but felt that the interior needed more pizzazz, so he hired Raymond Loewy's office to redesign them. The task fell to Andrew Geller.

None of the building's developers were thrilled with the resulting aesthetics. It was not a pretty house, but it did impress the curious Soviets who visited it by the thousands. *Pravda* referred to the model home as the "Taj Mahal." The kitchen became the centerpiece in a heated debate between Soviet Premier Nikita Khrushchev and U.S. Vice President Richard Nixon. The resulting press coverage catapulted Herbert Sadkin's career, which translated into more work for the Raymond Loewy office.

As early as 1959, it was rumored that Sadkin had purchased a large tract of land in Montauk, New York, and was planning a Levittown-like development for Leisure. Sadkin approached the Loewy office about designing a beach house that could be built by the hundreds. The homes, dubbed Leisurama, would be sold through Macy's Department Store and come fully furnished—down to the toothbrush. The task of designing the home naturally fell to Geller, who had the most experience of anyone designing beach houses and knew the lay of the land intimately.

The initial designs that Geller produced reflected his tendency to break with convention. (**Fig. 6.5**) One rendering depicts a multi-tiered structure composed of grouped pods, each pod resembled an upside down cross section of a ship's hull, the roofline angling down to meet the ground. In one illustration the driveway runs along the shoreline, thereby doubling its function—as a place to park a car and a location to dock a boat. The nautical feel of the home was meant to appeal to the young, middle-class weekend fisherman and his small family.

Mr. Sadkin was hesitant to accept this concept, not because he didn't like the design, but because it would be too expensive to mass-produce. After the intense publicity he received as a result of his Soviet triumph, he was also concerned about producing something that would be deemed unbelievable by the average Russian citizen. Under intense pressure to conform to standards that the U.S. State Department demanded, Sadkin requested a more conventional design for his community of vacation homes. What he received were essentially three variations on a rectangular box, with a gabled roof and a carport. (Fig. 6.6)

Geller was disappointed in the restrictions placed on the design. He bemoaned what he called the "cell-like" confines of the little boxy structures that would dot the hills of Montauk's Culloden Shores. Still, a hint of his creative aesthetic managed to creep in. Every Leisurama house had cathedral ceilings. Every Leisurama house had a compact bathroom, often with hidden storage compartments. Years later many people would look back at their childhoods spent in the houses with great fondness because the interiors were fanciful, and there were a lot of great hiding spots.

Despite his reservations about the design of the houses, Geller marveled at the creative marketing genius behind the Leisurama project. Never before had one of his houses been built at full scale in a department store—a Leisurama model was constructed on the ninth floor of Macy's Herald Square store in New York City. He was also impressed with the enthusiasm that Raymond Loewy's public relations director Elizabeth Reese exhibited in promoting the project in conjunction with All-State Properties and Macy's efforts. Each home was delivered completely furnished, with every necessity for living. This concept alone made involvement in the project worthwhile for Geller.

During the time that Leisurama was being conceived and built, Geller was working furiously at night in his home office, producing one-of-a-kind vacation houses. He produced twelve unique structures between 1962 and 1965. Each more inventive and more unusual in appearance, than the one before. Yet they are always beautiful in form, symmetrical, peaceful. Elizabeth Reese's home on Brick Kiln Road in Bridgehampton celebrates the beauty of its wooded environment with two-story angular windows and a catwalk that leads to a loft in the trees. The Levitas House on the cliffs of Martha's Vineyard resembles a bird with folded wings, perched and ready to fly off into the ocean's horizon. (Fig. 6.2) Each structure seems to represent an escape from the convention Geller lived with during the day when he designed for less adventurous corporate clients.

Geller would design several tract home developments for the Loewy organization over the years. He retired from the Loewy office in 1975 but continued his freelance work, and he would often take on subcontracting projects from other firms. In this manner he was able to add to his list of accomplishments such projects as the New York World Trade Center's restaurants (including Windows on the World), and large public structures in countries such as Israel and Japan.

Over time, the Leisurama community in Montauk evolved. Although additions and other structural alterations were made to the exterior

6.5

Fig. 6.5—One of Geller's Leisurama concepts

6.6

Fig. 6.6—Approved design for the Convertible
Leisurama

6.7

of many homes, very few changes have been made to the interiors. In recent years Geller has enjoyed visiting the Leisurama development and delights in relating memories of the project to any interested listeners.

The Leisurama development has indeed withstood the test of time. Though a handful of oversized shingle-style homes have appeared in the neighborhood, completely out of style and context with their environment, the Leisurama houses predominate. This small region of Long Island's East End is still a reminder of the optimism found in a world embroiled in a cold war; there are not many neighborhoods in the Hamptons region of Long Island that can still boast that. Therefore, the Leisurama community is a precious resource worthy of recognition as historically significant and deserving of preservation.

---

This essay was based on numerous conversations the author, Jake Gorst, had with his grandfather, Andrew Geller.

Fig. 6.7—Andrew Geller, 1985

6.8

Fig.6.8—Convertible Leisurama now

Leisurama is
So Many
Things...

... a pleasure-packed tennis match

... a romp in the surf from your own private beach

use veranda

... a sun-filled poolside nap,
chat or game at the Surf and Cabana Club

... a stroll from Pool & Surf Club
along miles of scenic beaches

BUTTER

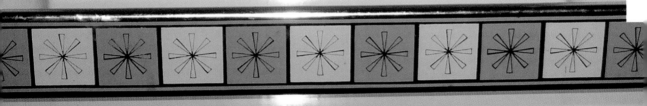

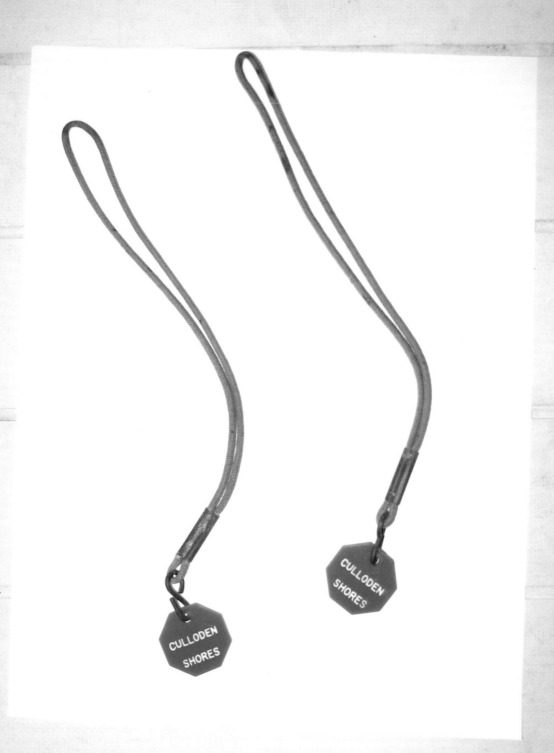

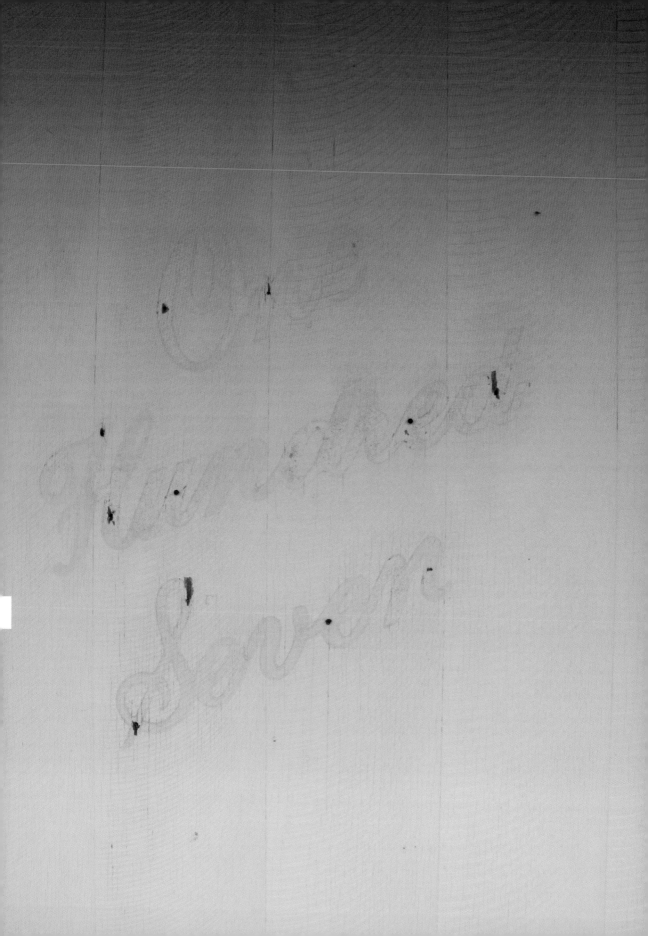

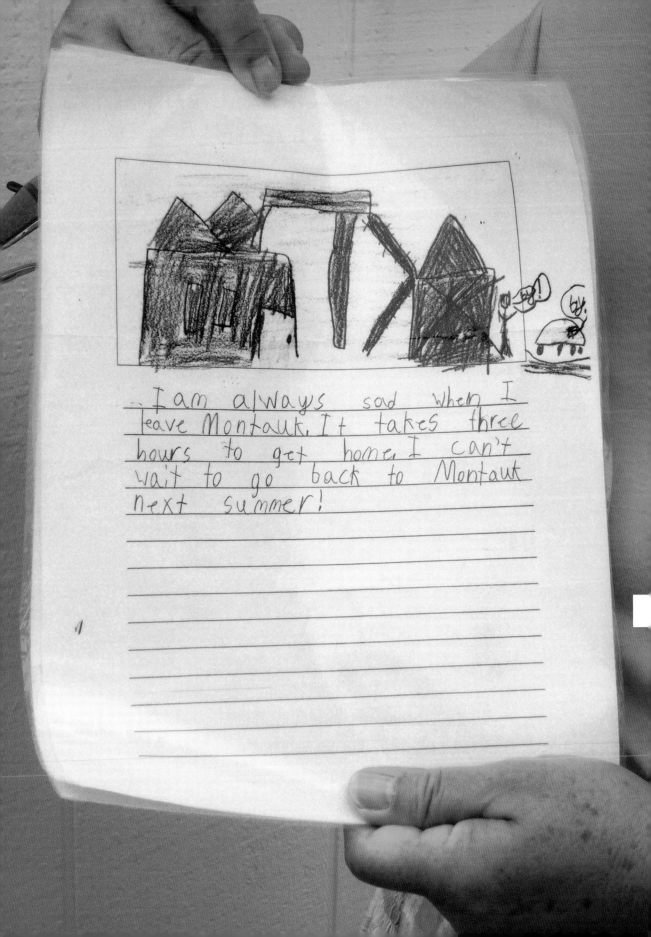

I am always sad when I leave Montauk. It takes three hours to get home. I can't wait to go back to Montauk next summer!

8.

# OWNING LEISURAMA

Paul Sahre

Murray and Laura Braverman's first introduction to Leisurama was in 1964. They were reading the *New York Times* late one Sunday evening, after putting their three children to bed. "We noticed an ad which read, 'Move into your new, fully furnished vacation home in Montauk.' Apparently, all you needed was $490 down," Murray Braverman remembers. (see page 236) The low price, an F.H.A. mortgage at 5.25 percent, and the attractive terms got them considering the possibility of owning a summer house. "We thought that the kids were just about old enough for summer camp and the notion that the house came fully furnished, down to the toothbrushes, was appealing. Especially to a dentist."

Distractions from family and a thriving dentistry practice delayed a decision until a chance trip to Macy's Herald Square. "I had an office between Thirty-sixth and Thirty-seventh streets at the time and we were needing to refurnish our waiting room. It was raining and our patients cancelled so we decided to walk over to Macy's. When we arrived, lo and behold, there was a big advertisement there for Leisurama which directed us to the ninth floor." Remembering the ad in the *New York Times*, Dr. Braverman and his office partner went straight there and were greeted by an actual, full-size model of the Convertible Leisurama. The rain had apparently kept the shoppers away, as they had five sales people all to themselves. "For $10, I left that day with a binder on four pieces of property in Montauk."

8.1

8.4

8.5

Fig. 8.1—Future site of the Braverman's Leisurama          Fig. 8.5–7—Endless summers in Montauk
Fig. 8.2–4—Nearing completion

8.2

8.3

NOV 64

8.7

8.6

Even factoring in the previous discussion with his wife, deciding to buy a summer house after a visit to a department store was the ultimate impulse buy. Especially when you consider that neither one of them had ever actually been to Montauk. But for Murray, this was an opportunity too good to be true. "After looking at the house and the layout, I thought that this was a great opportunity and that we'd get three of our friends to each buy a place, and we could all be neighbors and be out there together."

The fact he reserved four pieces of property speaks volumes about the lure of the Leisurama concept and price tag. "When you broke it down, the house and the land sold for $16,995 with an extra $995 for furniture and an extra $500 for the fireplace, unless you wanted beach front. Those were larger plots, and cost an extra $9,000. You could also buy individual plots for $3,500, so if you didn't want to put up a house you could still buy the land." Laura adds, "Our daughter Alisa, who was four at the time, said 'buy land daddy.'"

They had one week to make up their minds. The first thing they did was to visit Montauk and Culloden Shores. "We drove out on a Sunday in November. Back then the Long Island Expressway only went out to the Veterans Memorial Parkway, so you had to take the old Montauk Highway. We didn't know where we were going or how long it would take. We had never been out to Montauk in our entire lives and it was snowing." They were headed to a reception for prospective buyers at the Carl Fisher Building in the center of Montauk, which, because of its color and size, was nicknamed "The White Elephant." At six stories high, it was (and still is) the tallest building in Montauk. "After the reception, we had a salesman take us out to the property. The area was pristine, just gorgeous. There was a hill that sloped down to the beach, and there was nothing else there except deer feeding. He showed us the property and took us down to the water. We loved it."

Having satisfied themselves that their decision to buy a house from a department store was justified, they put down the $490 deposit, signed the contract, and met with the Macy's interior decorator. "They had four color schemes for the homes: blue, green, orange, and tan. The furniture came standard—with no options—but you could pick the color of the dishes and the countertops. You could order appliances that matched the rest of the kitchen, but they would take an extra six weeks to be delivered, so we went with white appliances," Laura remembers. The color scheme for each Leisurama was the only difference between houses. Otherwise, every Leisurama exterior was either a cool gray or a light yellow—except for the colored trim and doors, which matched the plates and kitchen countertops inside. **(Fig. 8.8)**

Seemingly, all that was left to do was wait and to look forward to their new life of leisure.

But that wasn't quite the way it worked out. During the winter of 1965, the Braverman family made several trips on the now familiar route to Montauk to check on the progress of the construction of their new house. They quickly found that progress was slow. "We would come out during the winter to see what was happening and nothing was going on. Once, we came out and were shocked to find the beautiful landscape our salesman had shown us had been flattened out. The excavation had started, and there were cinder blocks and pipes coming out of a large hole in the ground, and that

was it." Frustrated with the lack of progress, Murray remembered a discussion with a patient who was then the vice president of a company with an interest in bringing a department store out to the eastern tip of Long Island. "He wanted to know how the construction of the homes was progressing. I told him, 'What home? It's just a hole in the ground.'"

After the initial delay, construction momentum finally picked up. By April 30, 1965, the Bravermans were able to move in. "I think we came out on a Friday, and there was nothing in the house, the furnishings hadn't arrived yet. The Murphy Bed was there, so we put some sheets we brought with us over the windows, and we slept that first night in an empty house." The next day a Macy's truck delivered the furniture and furnishings, many of which required assembly. "We had a big bonfire going in the back yard that night with all of the boxes and wooden crates," recalls Mr. Braverman.

After settling in, Murray remembered a number of nagging construction issues they had to work through with the builder. This turned out to be a common occurrence, as many of their new neighbors were dealing with the same problems. (see pages 244–245) Another concern was the lack of landscaping provided by the builders. As it turned out, everything was included except landscaping and driveways, which left owners to their own devices. "They planted one tree and two bushes in every front yard. That was it. They also seeded each plot, but nothing they planted ever grew. So I ended up planting every blade of grass myself." To this day, there is a wonderful variety form yard to yard and driveway to driveway in Culloden Shores. (Fig. 8.9)

The Bravemans had three children between the ages of four and eight, so had their hands full. "In the beginning we could only make minor

Original color

Original color

Fig. 8.8—A sampling of non-original Leisurama
exterior colors and materials

(Original "lifetime guarentee" Redwood
siding from U.S. Plywood in the original color
options indicated)

8.9

Fig. 8.9—There are 161 Leisuramas remaining
in Culloden Shores, and there are almost as
many distinctive driveways.

Original entrance

8.10

Fig. 8.10—Changes to the front entrance
(original front entrance indicated)

8.11

Fig. 8.11—Landscaping not included

8.12

Fig. 8.12—Alterations to the Leisurama carport

changes. The first thing we did was put a window in the kitchen because it was so dark. We also had the shed enlarged. With three kids came bicycles and a lot of other stuff."

Since the houses were nearly identical and almost on top of each other, most Leisurama owners tried to find ways to create a semblance of privacy and individuality. "At first, you could walk into someone else's house and not even realize it wasn't yours; it was a natural mistake," jokes Murray. All manner of shrubbery and fencing began to appear in the neighborhood, and this has continued unabated up to the present. (Fig. 8.11)

Still, some have fond memories of the open, communal feeling of the original neighborhood. "I remember waking up in the morning and going out the back and walking across yards to my friend's house—the Solomons—who lived right on the corner across from the Jurichs. I could see their house from my backyard. I could also walk straight to the pond, so as kid it was great," says the Bravermans' daughter Alisa, who is now married with a family of her own. "Now you can't do that because most of the yards are fenced off."

But despite all of the effort, the majority of Leisuramas were still only a few yards from the next, just as they are today. She continues, "Even now, if our neighbors are out on their patio, we can hear everything they say, so while you can create the illusion of privacy, it's really not that private."

One of the first structural changes to appear in the neighborhood involved the trellis-like pergola. Initially, the pergola was a purely decorative ceiling of sturdy open cross beams that connected the main house to the shed. This created a carport for each Leisurama. Some owners converted them into garages, others used them for decks, and some created crow's nests that could provide an ocean view (which many expected when they first put down their deposits). (Fig. 8.12) The Bravermans eventually fenced off the carport and converted it into a patio. The pergola remains, though they recently had it rebuilt to match the original.

One of Leisurama's strongest (and unusual) selling points was good design at an affordable price. Walking through Culloden Shores today, one does not get the sense that there was much consideration in maintaining the integrity of the original design. The Braverman family is one of the few exceptions. Laura appreciated the design of the house and tried to preserve the original aesthetic when changes were made. "When we needed more space and we wanted to add another room, we didn't want to compromise the design of the house. It was very important to us that the house always look just the way it did. When we added a room, we did it so that it can't be seen from the front, so the house still looks original."

Throughout most of the neighborhood, however, practicality triumphed over aesthetics. One common example of this was many owners' decision to close off the front entrance area to create a vestibule. This seemed to make sense—it offered the opportunity for guests to enter into a smaller space and not directly into the living room, and it also solved an irritating flaw in the original Leisurama. The furnace was located directly behind vented double doors in this area, and on a windy day the pilot light would continually be blown out. This then required a trip out into the cold, sometimes in the middle of the night, to relight it. Regrettably, this alteration, as well as a number of others, transformed the look of the home from "beach house" to "suburban ranch." (Fig. 8.10)

8.13

Fig. 8.13—Murray and Laura Braverman and
their Leisurama, 2007

Another inadequacy that numerous owners complained of was the lack of natural light in the interior. This was remedied in many cases by the installation of skylights. "The house was too dark—it has a wooden cathedral ceiling and all of that wood paneling, so we installed skylights, and it wasn't long before some of our neighbors started doing the same. We replaced the windows throughout the house as well." Laura says. "The original windows were wooden, double-hung windows and there were plastic tracks that allowed for the the window to remain open at different heights, and out here they just rotted away, so you never knew if they would stay up, and they also began to warp. At a certain point they had to be replaced." Dr. Braverman concludes.

Over the years, creating additional space was the most common motivation for change, and this need has been satisfied in a variety of ways. Because the lots were so small (75 by 100 feet), owners typically built up. Changes to the original redwood exterior siding (which ironically came with a "lifetime guarantee" from U.S. Plywood) were also prevalent. While initially all of the Leisurama exteriors were redwood, dozens of different colors and materials can be spotted covering the exteriors today. (Fig. 8.8)

These changes are now the most fascinating aspect of the modern Leisurama community. While the original Leisurama lifestyle boasted the ultimate in convenience as a Leisurama ad promised, "just turn the key and start living," once the homes were purchased, owners spent a lot of time (and money) changing them. Perhaps all of that work was, and still is, inevitable. Alisa sums it up this way, "It's interesting that people didn't really want the convenience in the end. My father still makes changes and improvements to the house every year. He just enjoys it."

Over the last forty years, the alterations at Culloden Shores have not been confined to the houses. The neighbors have also changed. "My wife and I go to the beach because we love to swim, and we love the salt water, but now we don't recognize anyone. We used to have our own group, we would sit and kid around, and in the evenings we would go out to eat. Not anymore." Alisa agrees, "Up until I was in my twenties, the same families were here every year. I had my friends at home in Queens and I had my friends in Montauk. As I got older, I would work in the local restaurants with them, and everyone would be here for the whole summer." But it seems that this is no longer the case. "Few families spend the entire summer here anymore. Today it seems as if everyone's world is so scheduled and compartmentalized. It's unfortunate. The kids don't know the feeling of those endless summer days."

When asked if they would ever sell their Leisurama, Murray hedged, "I don't know. This house could go for $675,000. Can you believe it?" But any idea of selling was quickly squashed by Laura. "Just the other day, our granddaughter Rebecca [Alisa's daughter, age nine] said, 'Grandma don't ever sell this house.' When I asked her why, she replied, 'Because it's special.'"

---

This essay is based on an interview with Dr. Murray and Laura Braverman and their daughter Alisa Braverman, which was conducted in the summer of 2007.

# THEN AND NOW

Leisuramas relocated, obscured, gone

(A RE-PHOTOGRAPHIC STUDY)

## PHOTO INDEX

Fig. 9.1.1—Then: Expanded Convertible model on the Montauk Circle, 1964

Fig. 9.1.2—Now

Fig. 9.2.1—Then: Villa unit model on the Montauk Circle, 1964

Fig. 9.2.2—Now

Fig. 9.3.1—Then: Convertible model on the Montauk Circle, 1964

Fig. 9.3.2—Now

Fig. 9.4.1—Then: New York World's Fair, Court of the Moon, 1964 (Leisurama location indicated by arrow)

Fig. 9.4.2—Now

Fig. 9.5.1—Then: New York World's Fair, Lunar Fountain, 1964
(Leisurama location indicated by arrow)

Fig. 9.5.2—Now

Fig. 9.6.1—Then: Leisurama, Pinetree Drive, Culloden Shores, 2004

Fig. 9.6.2—Now

Fig. 9.7.1—Then: Leisurama, Bayberry Road, Culloden Shores, 2004

Fig. 9.7.2—Now

Fig. 9.8.1—Then: Backyard, Culloden Shores, 1965

Fig. 9.8.2—Now

Fig. 9.9.1—Then: Macy's Herald Square, 1964

Fig. 9.9.2—Now

# NOTES

## THE CIRCLE IN MONTAUK

PLATES 9.1–3 According to Frank Tuma, the Montauk Beach Company—a subsidiary of All-State Properties, for which he served as general sales manager and "approved any and all Leisurama sales"— was sold at some point in 1965 and was eventually dissolved. Few records for the Leisurama project still exist. Nonetheless, some documentation—including these three photographs—have found their way to the Montauk Library Archives. There is no information indicating who took the photographs, or when or why they were taken.

There is, however, plenty of anecdotal evidence that these are photographs of the three Leisurama sales models that originally stood on the circle in the center of town. These look like professionally produced photographs that were probably taken for some long-forgotten commercial or documentary purpose. There is concrete evidence in the images that not only firmly places each at the circle, but also indicates that they are Leisurama sales models (built by Ed Pospisil) and not the production homes (built later by Monvent).

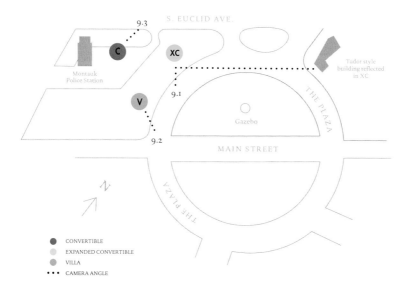

CONVERTIBLE
EXPANDED CONVERTIBLE
VILLA
CAMERA ANGLE

PLATE 9.1 The landscape behind the building in this photograph was not much help in determining the original location of this Expanded Convertible. Furthermore, there is no caption or label on the front or the back of this image. However, upon closer inspection, the reflection of a distinctive Tudor-style building (which still stands at the northeast corner of the circle) is clearly visible in the front window of this Leisurama. The general area in which these three Leisuramas are said to have been built is the present location of a small shopping center building on the northwest area of the circle (which is the current location of Pospisil Real Estate). Since there are no Leisuramas on the circle today, this location was verified by the reflection of the same Tudor-style building in the windows of the modern structure (below).

9.1.1 (detail)—Then, 1964     9.1.2 (detail)—Now

PLATE 9.2    The precise location of the Villa model on the Montauk Circle proved to be the most elusive. Visual inspection of the original photograph provided few clues, as did interviews with Frank Tuma and Ed Pospisil. Neither remember the exact location, and only generally remember that it faced the circle, as did the Expanded Convertible, that it was on the northwest side of the circle. The Pospisil construction sign in the foreground of the image indicates that this was a sales model. (Mr. Pospisil remembers building only one Villa, and that it was on the circle). The location I have settled on was suggested by the recollections of Mr. Pospisil and others as well as the curve of the sidewalk at the bottom of the original image, which seems to place this building on the west side of the circle intersecting Main Street.

PLATE 9.3    Of the three photographs of the Leisurama models, this was the only one which had any informa- tion on it. A caption, which was handwritten below the photograph, reads:

"B. BORIN #10 (746) LEISURAMA/POLICE STATION ED POSPISIL'S
OLD REAL ESTATE OFFICE CIRCA LATE 60's EARLY 70's."

This caption provided a starting point in determining the original location of this Convertible Leisurama despite the fact that it is incorrect. The Montauk police station is a small building a block from the circle and was, for a time, Ed Pospisil's old real estate office. Upon visual inspec- tion however—despite some similarities—this building is not a Leisurama. This was verified by Mr. Pospisil, who insists that his real estate office was originally housed in a Techbuilt House that his company constructed after Leisurama.

9.3.1 (details)—1964                9.3.2 (detail and alt. view)—2007

Examination of the photograph clearly places this Leisurama downtown. Its exact location was determined by two features in the original photograph. Despite the amount of changes to this area since 1964, a chimney on the left remains, as does a building and electric pole to the right, which is hidden from the original camera angle by the police station in the modern photograph.

Mr. Pospisil recalls that all three models originally located on the circle were sold and moved to other locations in Montauk.

# THE 1964–65 NEW YORK WORLD'S FAIR

PLATES 9.4-5    All-State Properties built two Leisuramas the New York World's Fair in 1964 on the northwest portion of the fairground on an avenue called "Court of the Moon." The fairgrounds have long since been converted to a park—virtually all of the structures were demolished or moved—but the original layout of the avenues and sidewalks is still in place. With the help of an original World's Fair map, it was very easy to find the location of the original All-State exhibit.

Ed Pospisil, who was hired by All-State to build the three Leisurama models on the circle in Montauk, also built the two buildings at the World's Fair. One was a Convertible model that had been designed for the Montauk development and the other was for a second development All- State had planned for Lauderhill, Florida.

It is interesting to note that of the numerous collections of World's Fair images, I could find images that included the Leisurama models, but only as peripheral subject matter. It is no won- der that these small and modest houses would have demanded little or no attention from photographers (professional and amateur alike). As you can see in plates 9.4–5, the All-State exhibition lot was tiny (75 feet by 100 feet, the same size as many of the residential lots in Montauk) and these two Leisuramas were dwarfed by their spectacular neighbors: Coca-Cola on one side and Seven-Up on the other.

Mr. Pospisil has no recollection of the fate of these two models.

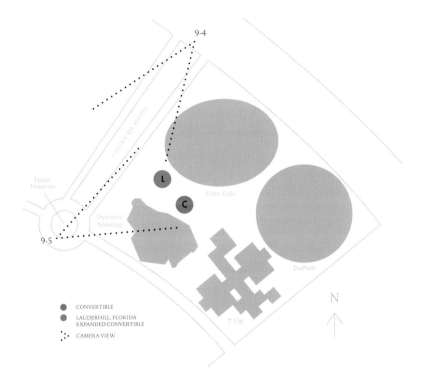

## CULLODEN SHORES

PLATES 9.6-8    Along with the sales models on the circle in Montauk, at the World's Fair, and at Roosevelt Field (below), a number of Leisuramas have been moved or torn down in Culloden Shores. Due to the lack of existing records, is was impossible to determine exact numbers.

Expanded Convertible, Roosevelt Field, 1963

We can report that in Culloden Shores, exactly three Leisuramas were torn down to make way for larger, modern homes from the time we began our photographic documentation (2004), to the date this book was published (2008). In addition, countless renovations to Leisuramas—some large, some small—occurred during this same period of time.

PLATE 9.8    The most noticeable difference in the neighborhood is the effects of forty years of individual landscaping efforts on the part of the Leisurama owners.

PLATE 9.9

On the 9th floor of the Macy's store in Herald Square—just off the century-old wooden escalator—is the spot were a convertible Leisurama sales model once stood. You can't shop for a house there today, but you can contemplate the fall of communism while you buy a new bedroom set. The area is—as it was then—the home furnishings department.

## A FINAL ACCOUNTING

Frank Tuma states that exactly 200 "production" homes were built in Montauk (this number does not include any of the sales models). Charles Piser's company, Monvent, built these Leisuramas in various neighborhoods in Montauk where All-State Properties owned land. Outside of the main development at Culloden Shores, there were a handful of Leisuramas built on Fort Hill near the Montauk Manor, in Hither Hills, and in Ditch Plains. There was also one Leisurama built in downtown Montauk—on the corner of South Elmwood Avenue and South Edison Street—which was originally zoned for commercial use (and still is). This Leisurama was built for Doris Lauter—the sister of Robert Lauter, then Macy's senior vice president of home merchandise—as a dress shop that she would own and operate for more than three decades. It is now a surf shop.

By our count, there are 187 Leisuramas remaining in Montauk today (162 of them are in Culloden Shores).[†] When one considers that scoffing critics predicted these homes would blow over after only a few years, this low attrition rate is proof of how well they were designed and built, and how much their owners appreciate them—then and now.

Facts attributed to Frank Tuma and Ed Pospisil are based on interviews that were conducted in the summer of 2007.

† This total is based on door-to-door verification.

# APPENDIXES

_____

## A. DOCUMENTS

## B. AFTERWORD

## C. LEISURAMA MODELS

## D. MAP

## E. CONTRIBUTORS, ACKNOWLEDGMENTS, CREDITS

DOCUMENT—I
Preliminary Plan of Premises
Culloden Shores

DATE_____

GENTLEMEN:

☐ YES...I am interested in learning more about LEISURAMA and how I can
   get more enjoyment and greater leisure pleasure.

☐ I would like to learn how I might possibly own this home and have it pay for
   itself!

☐ I would like to see LEISURAMA at Montauk, L.I.

Mr.
Mrs._____ Phone No._____

Address_____

City_____ Zone_____ State_____

## Leisurama

*Created by:* ALL-STATE PROPERTIES INC.

*Designed by:* Raymond Loewy/William Snaith, Inc.

*Decorated and furnished by:* MACY'S

## Macy's is proud to be part of this new way to enjoy your life of leisure

**DOCUMENT—II A/B**
Leisurama Reply Card and Sales Poster (FRONT)

(Following page)
**DOCUMENT—II C**
Leisurama Sales Poster (BACK, DETAIL)

... a breathtaking Montauk sunset

... a visit to Montauk Point Park and Lighthouse

... a bright morning of surf casting

... an exhilarating horseback ride

... a romp in the surf from your own private beach

... a pleasure-packed tennis match

... relaxation on the Club House veranda

... a challenging round of golf the famed Montauk Downs course

... the family boating and fishing life

# Leisurama is so many things ...

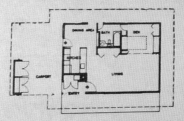

The CONVERTIBLE—This is the basic LEISURAMA home, priced at $12,990 on a 75x100-foot plot, including furniture, furnishings and appliances. Qualified buyers pay $490 down and $73* monthly, for interest as well as amortization and F.H.A.† insurance.

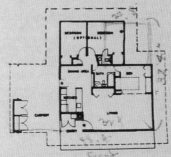

The EXPANDED CONVERTIBLE—This larger model adds two bedrooms and a powderroom to the basic plan. Priced at $15,990 on a 75x100-foot plot, including furniture, furnishings and appliances. For qualified buyers it is available for as little as $940 down and $87.90* monthly for interest as well as amortization and F.H.A.† insurance.

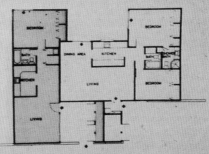

The VILLA—Designed for families who prefer trying LEISURAMA life on a rental basis, it contains two fully furnished and equipped suites. Villas will be built in waterfront clusters. One-bedroom unit rents for $1,600 a year, two-bedroom suite for $1,900.

\* includes furniture carrying charges
† F. H. A. financing on land and building

...ated by: ALL-STATE PROPERTIES INC.
...gned by: Raymond Loewy/William Snaith, Inc.
...riors by: MACY'S

South Mall opp. Macy's Auto Center.
Roosevelt Field • Montauk at East Hampton, L. I.

# MONTAUK BEACH CO

152 WEST 42nd STREET, NEW YORK 36, N. Y. • LO 5-7670

Subsidiary of

## ALL-STATE PROPERTIES

## Leisurama

Furniture, Equipment and Appliance

### INVENTORY

(Schedule A)

### FURNITURE AND FURNISHINGS

| | CONVERTIBLE (Cash Sale Price $540.) | EXPANDED CONVERTIBLE Two Bedroom (Cash Sale Price $940.) | Fabric Choice | Color Choice |
|---|---|---|---|---|
| Sofabed (Double Size) | 1 | 1 | x | x |
| Rectangular End Table | 1 | 1 | | |
| Round End Table | 1 | 1 | | |
| Small Cocktail Table | 1 | 1 | | |
| Club Chairs | 2 | 2 | x | x |
| Drop-Leaf Dining Table | 1 | 1 | | |
| Side Chairs | 5 | 5 | | |
| Lamps | 3 | 8 | | |
| Rug 6 x 9 | 1 | 1 | | x |
| Drapery-Living Room | 1 pr. | 1 pr. | x | x |
| Drapery-Sleeping Area | 1 pr. | 1 pr. | x | x |
| Drapery-Dinette Area | 1 pr. | 1 pr. | x | x |
| Dinette Set | 5 pcs. | 5 pcs. | | |
| Double Dressers and Mirrors | | 2 | | |
| Night Tables | | 3 | | |
| Double Headboards | | 2 | | |
| Boxspring and Mattress Sets | | 2 | | |
| Bedspreads | | 2 | | x |
| Side Chairs-Bedroom | | 2 | | |
| Drapery-Bedroom | | 4 pr. | x | x |
| Melmac Dinner Service for 8 | 45 pcs. | 45 pcs. | | x |
| Set of Plastic Glasses | 24 pcs. | 24 pcs. | | x |
| Stainless Flatware Service for 8 with Chest | 50 pcs. | 50 pcs. | | |
| Set of Aluminum Cookware | 7 pcs. | 7 pcs. | | |
| Plastic Place Mats | 8 | 8 | | x |
| Napkins | 8 | 8 | | x |
| Bath Towels | 4 | 8 | | x |
| Hand Towels | 4 | 8 | | x |
| Wash Cloths | 4 | 8 | | x |
| Shower Curtain | 1 | 1 | | x |
| Tub Mat | 1 | 1 | | x |
| Sheets | 8 | 16 | | |
| Pillow Cases | 8 | 16 | | |
| Summer Blankets, Double | 2 | 4 | | x |
| Dacron Pillows | 4 | 8 | | |

### APPLIANCES AND BUILT-IN EQUIPMENT
(included in both models)

G.E. Heating Unit

G.E. Range and Oven

G.E. Dishwasher

G.E. Refrigerator

G.E. Combination Washer-Dryer

Kitchen Cabinets

Plumbing and Heating Plants and Fixtures

Built-in "Phantom Bed"

Built-in Dressing Table

Electrical Ceiling Fixtures

# How to Use and Care for your
## GENERAL ELECTRIC AUTOMATIC
# Dishwasher

SD200, SD300, SC500 AND SC600 SERIES

**General Electric**
# RANGES
## User's Manual

❶ Calrod® Surface Units—Trim Rings—Reflector Pans

❷ No-drip Cooktop

❸ *Appliance Outlet

❹ Oven Set

❺ Oven Temp

❻ Oven Cycling Light

❼ Pushbutton Switches for Surface Units

❽ Master Indicating† Light for Surface Units

❾ *Automatic Timer— Clock—Minute Timer

❿ Calrod Broil Unit and Broil Reflector

⓫ Oven Light

⓬ Sliding Oven Shelves

⓭ Broiler Pan and Rack

⓮ Tilt-Lock Calrod Bake Unit

⓯ Removable Oven Door

⓰ Fan and Light Switch

⓱ Circuit Breaker or Fuse

*Except JM61; JM62

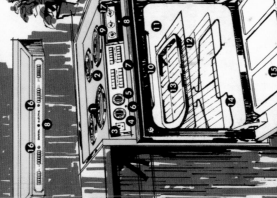

(Top)
**DOCUMENT—V**
G.E. Dishwasher User's Manual

(Bottom)
**DOCUMENT—VI**
G.E. Electric Range User's Manual

238
239

# WESTERN UNION
## TELEGRAM
W. P. MARSHALL, PRESIDENT

SF-1201 (4-60)

The filing time shown in the date line on domestic telegrams is LOCAL TIME at point of origin. Time of receipt is LOCAL TIME at point of destination

3 21P EDT MAY 20 65 PB225

SYE248 SY BEA058 PD ISLIP NY 20 253P EDT

RAY JURICH

  229 LINCOLN AVE ELIZABETH NJER

LEISURAMA CLOSING SET FOR MAY 26 PLEASE CONFIRM IMMEDIATELY

CALL JU 1-4505

  JOEL S JABLON MONVENT INC.

*516 - Junipos?*

*28 May*

(Above)
**DOCUMENT—VII**
Telegram from Joel S. Jablon, Monvent,
to Ray Jurich

(Right)
**DOCUMENT—VIII**
Contract for the Purchase
of a Leisurama Lot 224

# Contract

**Agreement** made and dated this **16** day of **March** 1964, between MONTAUK BEA[CH COMPA]
NY, a domestic corporation having an office at 230 Park Avenue, New York City 17, New York, hereinafter described as [the seller]

**Ray V. Jurich**                  and                  **Tina Jurich**                  his [wife]

[resid]ing at **229 Lincoln Avenue, Elizabeth, N.J.** hereinafter described as the purcha[ser]

**Witnesseth** That the seller agrees to sell and convey, or cause to be conveyed, and the purchasers agree to purchas[e a]
[a] parcel of land with the buildings and improvements thereon erected or to be erected, situate, lying and being in Montauk, [East Hampton]
Township, County of Suffolk and State of New York, more particularly described as follows:

[Lot] No. **224** in Block No. _____, on Map of **Culloden Shores**
[N]o. **2**, bearing Map No. _____, in the office of the County Clerk, Suffolk County, New York, located on [the]
_____ side of _____ being approximately **75' x100'** feet in dimensions and known as Seller's
_____, Model **Expanded Convertible with Fireplace**

[TO]GETHER with an easement over the streets to the nearest public highway, but excepting and reserving the fee to the said str[eets]
[the fee] of which is not hereby conveyed.

[TH]E DEED SHALL BE IN PROPER STATUTORY FORM for record; shall contain such a description of the premises as [is requir]-
[requir]ed by the lending institution and/or title company insuring said lender; shall be Bargain and Sale, with covenant against gran[tor];
[and] shall be duly executed and acknowledged by the seller at the seller's expense, so as to convey to the purchaser the fee simp[le to the]
[said] premises, free of all encumbrances except as herein stated. The said deed shall also contain the covenant required by Subdivisi[on]
[Sectio]n 13 of the Lien Law and all amendments thereto.

[The p]urchasers represent that they have inspected and are familiar with the model house. If the construction of the dwelling sold herei[n has]
[comm]enced or is in the course of construction, it is to be substantially similar to the Model House; Type, _____ ; shall be [built]
[in] accordance with municipal requirements and requirements of the lending institution which shall make the mortgage loan; an[d in accordan]-
[c]e with the plans and specifications as filed with the governmental authorities. Included in this sale are the following as shown i[n the model]
[ho]use: (a) Range; (b) Dishwasher; (c) Refrigerator; (d) Combination Washer-Dryer; (e) Kitchen cabinets; (f) Plumbing and he[ating]
[and] fixtures; (g) Built-in "Phantom Bed"; (h) Built-in dressing table; (i) electrical fixtures. The furniture, furnishings and equip[ment]
[with]in and landscaping around, the model house are not included in the sale except as specified herein to the contrary. Title to all ar[ticles]
_____ [s]hall be delivered free and clear of all encumbrances save and except the lien of the mortgage h[erein]
_____ [app]liances and Purchaser agrees to make selections w[ithin]

[Ri]der "A" attached to agreement dated **March 16, 1964**, between Montauk Beach
[Com]pany, Inc., as Seller, and Ray V. Jurich and Tina Jurich
[as] Purchaser.

[Th]e lot described herein is located on a preliminary map which has been submitted for
[app]roval by the Town Planning Board for filing in the Office of the County Clerk.

[ ... ]

[ ... ] [title] closing; (e) covenants, agreements an[d ... ]
[existe]nce of the structures referred to herein; (f) protective covenants and restrictions imp[osed ... ]
[property] herein described, provided same are not more onerous than those required by the FHA and, protective covenants and restric[tions]
[impos]ed by the FHA or lending institution to run with the land and to be recorded as a blanket encumbrance against the area of w[hich the]
[prop]erty herein is a part; (g) approval by governing local authorities, building department, zoning board, board of appeals, and pla[nning]
[ ] commission as to building, plot layout and/or subdivision of acreage, if a subdivision map is not filed.
_____ [p]ayable as follows:

CONTRACT OF SALE OF HOUSE
152 West 42nd Street
New York 36, N. Y.
LO 5-7670

MONTAUK BEACH COMPANY
(A subsidiary of All State Properties)
MONTAUK, LONG ISLAND
HOUSING DIVISION

# Contract

with

Builders' Job No.

Building Department

TOWN OF EAST HAMPTON

# CERTIFICATE OF OCCUPANCY

No. _____3266_____        Date _February 16,_____, 1965

THIS CERTIFIES that the building located at _Butternut Drive_____

~~Street~~ _Culloden Shores, Montauk_____, Block No. ___-_____, Lot No. ___224___
                  (Village)

Map No. _____4019_____, conforms substantially to the approved plans and

specifications heretofore filed in this office with Application for Building Permit date

____July 2,_____, 19_64_, pursuant to which Building Permit No. ___3266____

dated ____July 2,_____, 19⁶⁴ was issued, and conforms to all of the requirements

of the applicable provisions of the law. The occupancy for which this certificate is

issued is _1036 sq. ft. one-story, one-family residence, 194 sq. ft. deck and_
          _363 sq. ft. carport._

This certificate is issued to _____MONVENT, Inc. ( CS2-0-224-ECF )_____
                          (owner, ~~lessee or tenant~~)

of the aforesaid building.

*Norman Quarty*

FORM 3                        Senior    Building Inspector
                                  NORMAN QUARTY

# Monvent, Inc.

### BUILDERS OF LEISURAMA HOMES

**OLD MONTAUK HIGHWAY**
**MONTAUK POINT, L. I., NEW YORK**

June / , 1965

Mr. and Mrs. Ray V. Jurich
229 Lincoln Avenue
Elizabeth, New Jersey

Re: Monvent Job No. CS2-0-224

Dear Mr. and Mrs. Jurich:

In connection with the closing of title to the above captioned
premises which took place today, please be advised that for
the period commencing today and ending on June / , 1966,
we hereby guarantee the plumbing and heating systems, amd
the roof and foundation installed at said premises against all
defects in material and construction and installation.

Very truly yours,

MONVENT, INC.

By_____
Murray Bogatin, Assistant Secretary

DOCUMENT—X
Letter from Murray Bogatin, Monvent,
to Mr. and Mrs. Jurich

Murray Bogatin, Esq.                                    April 17th, 1965
309 Main Street
Islip, New York

Re: Job. No. CS2-O-224 ECF, Montauk, N.Y.

Dear Mr. Bogatin:

Last Sunday my wife and I again made a trip to Montauk to
inspect our future home. What we found was more than disap-
pointing.

Since our last inspection in February, as reported in my
letter of March 17th, only three items were handled: door
bell was installed, broken louvered door was replaced on the
outside storage closet, and the stuck windows were loosened.

Enclosed is a list of items which must be taken care of.
The house must then be cleaned before the furnishings could
be brought in.

I am quite displeased with the manner in which this project
has been handled, and particularly with the unreasonable delay
in its completion. According to my contract, the home was to
be completed by June of 1964. The failure to do so has already
cost me a considerable sum of money as I had to make alternate
vacation arrangements last summer for my family. We are now
almost one year later. Such delay could not possibly be called
"reasonable". On the contrary. I doubt that in a court of law
anyone would dispute a claim that it constitutes a breach of
contract.

I must insist that you instruct the builders to complete
the work immediately. When you have their assurance that it
has been done, please confirm it to me in writing, as I can not
afford to invest time again into fruitless 300-mile trip.

Kindly be on notice that my family and I intend to move into
the house as early as possible in May; if the house is not
completed fully and to our satisfaction by May 15th I shall
consider it a breach of contract.

                                    Sincerely yours,


                                    Ray V. Jurich

RVJ/s
Enc.: list

<u>Linen closets</u> (3 – one in area between kitchen and bedroom
one in bathroom
one next to Phantom Bed)

All shelves to be replaced with shelves 3-4" deeper, except in
closet next to Phantom Bed where shelves should be exactly
doubled in width – in other words, shelves should be as deep
as closets allow.

<u>Clothes closets</u> (3 in sleeping areas
1 in living room)

Shelves above clothes bars to be replaced with considerably
deeper shelves to take advantage of full closet depth.

<u>Floor tiles</u>

Two tiles to be pasted under window in Phantom-bed room. In
same room, all tiles to be replaced in area where phantom bed
is stored (some are missing, others are mutilated).

<u>Patio</u> not finished

<u>Driveway</u> to be finished (carport area unfinished).

<u>Refrigerator</u> to be installed. Clean area before installation.

<u>Dishwasher</u> not properly installed.

<u>Ceiling light</u> in breakfast area to be installed

<u>Window</u> in living room, first on left as you enter front door,
to be replaced – ill fitting, large gap on runner on left side of
window.

<u>Light switch</u> which operates light in linen closet area between
kitchen and bedroom to be corrected; switch button crooked.

<u>Phantom Bed</u> to be installed.

<u>Accordion door track</u> to be installed – only half done.

<u>Range</u> – sliding metal panel on side of range to be secured (left side

<u>Heating unit</u> to be checked; thermostat in off position but heater
continues to turn on (temperature in room about 68°).

**DOCUMENT—XI B**
Letter from Leisurama Owner Ray V. Jurich
to Murray Bogatin Esq., Monvent
(Page 2)

244
245

MACY★S ★ NEW YORK

*A division of R. H. Macy & Co. Inc.*

EXECUTIVE OFFICES

HERALD SQUARE
NEW YORK, N.Y. 10001

Mr. Ray V. Jurich
229 Lincoln Ave.
Elizabeth, New Jersey

RE: CS-2-0-224ECF

With regard to the title closing of the subject premises between you and
Monvent, Inc. today, you are advised that Macy's has been paid by Monvent, Inc.
for the furniture and furnishings as listed in the order received by Macy's for
your house. Macy's will deliver the furniture and furnishings to you within a
period from 2 to 10 days from the date hereof (on a specific date to be agreed
upon).

You may be assured that the quality of the furniture and furnishings
which are being supplies by Macy's is up to our standards in all respects, and
that our usual service policies will prevail.

Very truly yours,

MACY'S NEW YORK
(Division of R. H. Macy & Co., Inc.)

*[signature]*

DELIVERY DATE 6/5      TIME 10:30

MACY'S HERALD SQUARE, THE WORLD'S LARGEST STORE ★ WHITE PLAINS ★ FLATBUSH ★ JAMAICA ★ PARKCHESTER ★ ROOSEVELT FIELD ★ HUNTINGTON ★ BAY SHORE

**DOCUMENT—XII**
Letter from Macy's to
Mr. Ray V. Jurich

HOW YOU CAN MAKE

*The* Magic of Montauk YOURS...

A verified statement, a[nd] offering [state]ment, ha[s] been file[d with] the De-partment [of State of] New Ya[rk... th]e filing does not [...] proval [...] lease or [...] or lease[...] the De[part]-ment of State or any officer thereof, or that the Department of State has in any way passed upon the merits [of su]ch offering. A copy [of the] offering statem[ent is] available upon [request] from the sub-divi[der.]

# Montauk
## ESTATES

- **OCEANSIDE AT MONTAUK**
- **SOUND VIEW ESTATES**
- **HITHER HILLS**

**DOCUMENT—XIII**
Montauk Estates Sales Kit (cover)

# GENERAL ⊕ ELECTRIC
## COMPANY

| | MAJOR APPLIANCE |
| | DIVISION |
| | PRODUCT SERVICE |

49-10 NORTHERN BOULEVARD, LONG ISLAND CITY 1, NEW YORK . . . TELEPHONE AStoria 4-5100 | METROPOLITAN NEW YORK AREA

October 18, 1965

Mr. Charles Piser
Building Ventures, Inc.
309 Main St.              Re:  Leasurama Homes
Islip, L. I., N. Y.                at Montauk

Dear Mr. Piser:

We have been working on several complaints of unbalanced heat in the Leasurama Homes and have found that they can be balanced in real good shape by the following procedure:

1. The furnace blower should be on slow speed.
2. The fan switch should be at 110° setting.
3. The furnace should be fired at its full Propane rating. #53 orifices ≠ 11" water pres.
4. A 10" round baffle with a 3" hole in its center should be installed in the register opening by the front door and pushed back toward the furnace about 4 or 5 inches.
5. Final distribution balance can be made at the individual registers.

Dave Strutt has been given a sample of the above referred to baffle and a set of heating layout plans with the above instructions.

In checking some of these homes, we found that some people have covered the furnace door louvers almost completely. It should be brought to the attention of these people that combustion air requirements for these furnaces and water heaters must comply with the standards of the National Board of Fire Underwriters and the American Gas Association. For these particular houses with a furnace rated at 105,000 BTU's and a water heater rated at 40,000 BTU's, there should be two openings from outdoors into the furnace room at top and bottom of not less than 46 square inches each.

If the combustion air was to be taken from inside the house, these openings would have to be 145 square inches each.

We certainly hope that the results of our investigation and our recommendations will be helpful to you in getting these complaints of inadequate heat in some of the rooms of these houses taken care of.

Mortgage Payment Book

SECURITY NATIONAL BANK
OF LONG ISLAND

Member Federal Reserve System • Federal Deposit Insurance Corporation

MORTGAGE DEPARTMENT

23157

---

SECURITY NATIONAL BANK
OF LONG ISLAND

MORTGAGE DEPARTMENT

13 23157

IF YOUR ADDRESS CHANGES—

WRITE YOUR NEW ADDRESS HERE

NAME

NEW ADDRESS

CITY & STATE

Please use this form to notify us immediately of any change in your address.

TELLERS STAMP

PAID STAMP INDICATES
RECEIPT OF PAYMENT
AS SHOWN ON
CORRESPONDING COUPON

IF PAID BY MAIL

---

## INSTRUCTIONS FOR MAKING PAYMENTS

**IN PERSON**

Present this book with payment at any office of the SECURITY NATIONAL BANK OF LONG ISLAND.

**BY MAIL**

Tear out coupon and send it with your remittance to SECURITY NATIONAL BANK, 350 Main St., Huntington, N.Y. DO NOT SEND THE ENTIRE BOOK.

If more than one payment is being made, send one coupon for each payment.

Your cancelled check or money order stub is your receipt for mail payments.

Make all remittances payable to SECURITY NATIONAL BANK OF LONG ISLAND.

**CHANGE OF ADDRESS**

Please notify us of a change of address, write your new address on the form in back of this book and mail it immediately.

**IMPORTANT**

Payments must be made in the exact amount and reach us on the due date designated on each coupon.

Promptness in meeting obligations establishes your credit standing, therefore, make it a practice to mail your payment to reach us on its due date.

Delinquency in payment of an installment results in additional expense to you in the form of late charges. Part payments cannot be accepted.

A statement of your account showing all payments and disbursements will be sent to you in January, as of December 31st of each year.

A new coupon book will be sent to you after the last coupon in your book has been used.

**DOCUMENT—XV**
Mortgage Payment Book

B.

# AFTERWORD

During a recent trip to Japan (unrelated to this book), I found myself daydreaming in the living room of a *ki no ie* (house of wood), on the ground floor of a Muji department store in Tokyo.

For the uninitiated, Muji is a department store chain that has often been referred to as the IKEA of Japan and is known for its simple, flexible, and well-designed products. I was standing in one such "product": a full-size model home designed by Kazuhiko Namba and completely furnished from top to bottom with everything from Muji. The house has the recognizable Muji price tag on the exterior—although at a much larger scale—just like all of the other products the department store sells.

There was no way I could have walked out of Muji that day with a house, but nonetheless, imagined sitting down with a sales person (and a translator), deciding on available options, and then putting down a deposit.

As it turns out, the Muji house does not come "as you see it" like the Leisurama did. But no big deal, I could simply get a really big shopping cart and head up to the second floor and buy everything à la carte.

I would have the house built on some beautiful, undeveloped land— near the ocean—a few hours from my home in Brooklyn. The furnishings would be delivered, and my wife and I would move into this house and we would keep everything exactly as it was and never change it. We would go for walks on the beach and stay up late on the hammock in the backyard looking at the sky.

We would start living our life of Leisure. That is, until someone built an identical Muji house across the street; then we would probably have to start changing everything. —*PS*

# C.

## *Leisurama Models*

### C

### THE CONVERTIBLE LEISURAMA
Basic model

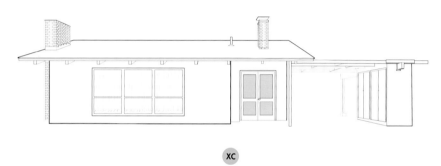

### XC

### THE EXPANDED-CONVERTIBLE LEISURAMA
Expanded model

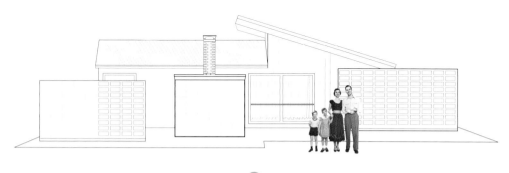

### V

### THE VILLA LEISURAMA
Rental suite

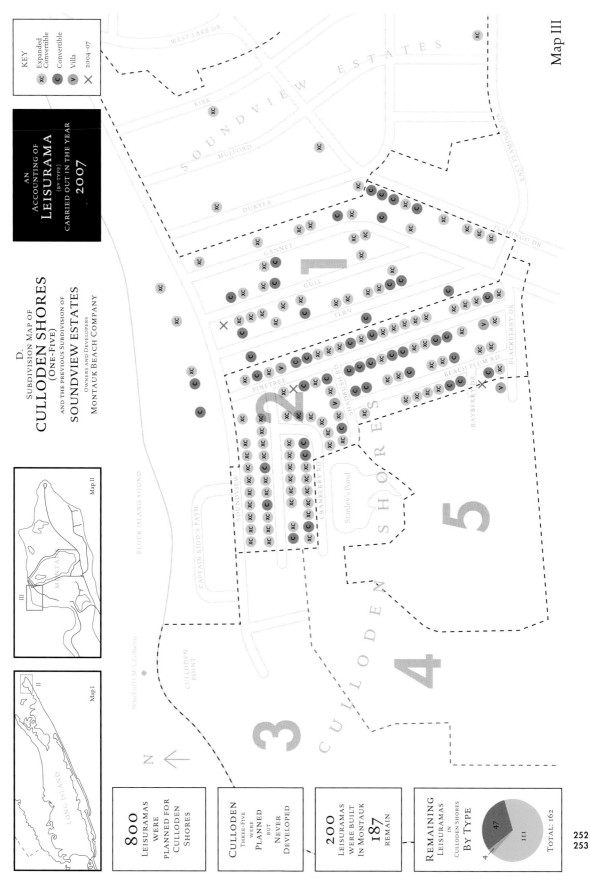

KEY

| | Expanded Convertible |
|---|---|
| XC | Convertible |
| V | Villa |
| X | 2004–07 |

AN
ACCOUNTING OF
LEISURAMA
(BY TYPE)
CARRIED OUT IN THE YEAR
2007

D.
SUBDIVISION MAP OF
CULLODEN SHORES
(ONE–FIVE)
AND THE PREVIOUS SUBDIVISION OF
SOUNDVIEW ESTATES
OWNERS AND DEVELOPERS
MONTAUK BEACH COMPANY

Map II

Map I

N

800
LEISURAMAS
WERE
PLANNED FOR
CULLODEN
SHORES

CULLODEN
THREE–FIVE
WERE
PLANNED
BUT
NEVER
DEVELOPED

200
LEISURAMAS
WERE BUILT
IN MONTAUK
187
REMAIN

REMAINING
LEISURAMAS
IN
CULLODEN SHORES
BY TYPE

TOTAL: 162

Map III

# E.

## CONTRIBUTORS

Paul Sahre is a graphic designer, educator, and author who works out of his own design office in New York City. He is the coauthor of *Hello World: A Life in Ham Radio*, a book based on a collection of QSL cards, which amateur radio enthusiasts exchange with other "Hams" around the world. He is also a frequent visual contributor to the *New York Times*.

William Morgan is an architectural historian and writer based in Rhode Island. The author of *The Abrams Guide to American House Styles* and *The Cape Cod Cottage*, he and his wife Carolyn restored a 1915 vicarage in Providence.

Jake Gorst is the Emmy Award–winning writer, producer, and director of the PBS documentaries *Leisurama* and *Farmboy* as well as owner of Jonamac Productions. Gorst is a regular contributing writer for *Modernism*, *Vox,* and *Home Miami* magazines.

For the past thirty-five years, Michael Northrup has been photographing everything around him through his odd and idiosyncratic lens. A book of his work, *Beautiful Ecstasy*, was published in 2003 by J+L Books. He lives in Baltimore, Maryland.

Peter J. Ahlberg is a graphic designer who works out of his own studio. He received a BFA from the School of Visual Arts, where he is now an adjunct professor. He lives in New York City with his wife.

## ACKNOWLEDGMENTS

In the process of making this book, I became aware that a documentary film about Leisurama was in production to be released in 2005. After getting over an initial feeling of disappointment, I purposely avoided the film, not wanting to be unduly influenced by it as I developed this book. As I probably knew then—it would only be a matter of time—that I would contact the filmmaker Jake Gorst for help. Jake's interest in Leisurama as the subject of a film was similar to mine even if his introduction to it was not. We both saw an opportunity to tell an interesting story, one which few knew or cared about outside of Montauk, but Jake's introduction to Leisurama was much less haphazard than my own—he is the grandson of the Leisurama's architect Andrew Geller. Jake could not have been more helpful and generous. I would like to take this opportunity to thank him for all of the shared information, photographs, and answers, and for agreeing to contribute an essay about his grandfather (page 179).

To all of the Lesiurama owners of whom, as a renter, I am very jealous: thank you for your hospitality, iced tea, and memories, and for allowing us to intrude with camera in hand. I would like to make special mention of Eileen and Ed Takayesu, my Leisurama landlords and facilitators, who assisted me in many ways; Laura and Dr. Murray Braverman and their daughter Alisa for their time, effort, and memories; Mia Certic and Jessica James for sharing some of their father's fastidious paperwork; and Marion Milcetic, Janet Micheline, Patricia O'Donnell, Ralph Barone, Tony Grafanino, David Goodman, Christine Orndahl, Evelyn Spiegler, and Leisurama and Memory Motel owner Arthur Schneider.

To the two "deans" of Montauk real estate, Frank Tuma and Ed Pospisil: thank you for agreeing to be interviewed and for discussing your involvement in Leisurama.

To current Pospisil real estate agents Margaret Harvey and Robert Cronley for their time and expertise. Also, thank you to Lexa Tuma Dispirito from The Tuma Agency for arranging an interview with her father, and to Janice Hayden from Coldwell Banker and the Tighe family for allowing us to tour the family home to document original Leisurama items and details.

To Robin Strong from the Montauk Library for her kind assistance with archive material. She has a great job.

To everyone at Princeton Architectural Press and especially to Deb Wood and my editor Jennifer Thompson.

To photographer and friend Michael Northrup for his numerous trips to Montauk to photograph many of the images represented in this book.

To William Morgan for agreeing to write a history of Leisurama, and for being a calming voice through out.

To Debbie Millman for helping me with the difficult task of writing, and for her enthusiastic support of this book.

Also, to Neri Schulman for the tour of her Leisurama shop and for finding me an original drop-leaf table.

To Jason Fulford who helped to get this project off the ground.

To Joseph and Adrienne Bresnan for their encouragement and advice.

To Bill Cotter for researching his '64 World's Fair collection for images of Leisurama and for his kind permission to reproduce a number of them.

To Joanna Berman for help with photo researching.

To Akiko Sakai, my former intern who served as translator at the Muji store in Tokyo.

To Cas Foglia of the Culloden Shores Association for resolving that parking issue.

To Nicholas Blechman, Brian Rea, Sarah Swanson, Christoph Niemann, Lisa Zeitz, and Sid who shared most of that first Montauk summer with me.

To my design assistants: Andrea Koch, Loren Flaherty, Michiel van Wijngaarden, Jonathan Han, Ulrike Schwach. Also to Robey Clark and Shawn Hasto for their special guest appearances.

Finally, to Peter Ahlberg, my main collaborator on this book, who helped in all facets of its creation. He designed, he organized, he traveled, he photographed, he transcribed, and he drank iced tea.

## CREDITS

All images by the Office of Paul Sahre (Paul Sahre, Peter Ahlberg, Andrea Koch, Loren Flaherty, Jonathan Han and Michiel van Wijngaarden), unless otherwise noted.

Page 16 (1.8)
AP Photo

Pages 172 (8.1, 8.2, 8.3, 8.4, 8.5, 8.6, 8.7)
Courtesy of the Braverman Family

Pages 28 (1.22), 34 (1.25), 226 (9.9.1), 229,
234–40, 242–49, 251
Courtesy of Mia Certic and Jessica James

Pages 218 (9.4.1), 220 (9.5.1)
From the collection of
Bill Cotter

Pages 18 (1.10), 24 (1.12, 1.13, 1.14), 171 (6.1),
172 (6.2, 6.4), 178 (6.5), 180 (6.7)
Courtesy of Andrew Geller

Page 172 (6.3)
Courtesy of Andrew Geller,
Photo by Jerry Birnbaum

Pages 14 (1.6), 28 (1.23)
Courtesy of Jake Gorst

Pages 184–85
Photos by John M. Hall

Pages 14 (1.5), 214 (9.1.1), 216–17
(9.2.1, 9.3.1)
Montauk Library

Page 14 (1.7)
National Archives and Records
Administration

Pages 11 (1.4), 87–168, 181 (6.8), 208 (8.13),
215 (9.1.2), 216–17 (9.2.2, 9.3.2), 219 (9.4.2),
221 (9.5.2), 222–23 (9.6.1–9.6.2, 9.7.1–9.7.2)
by Michael Northrup

Page 224 (9.8.1)
Courtesy of the Orndahl Family

Pages 49–58
Leisurama tour photographs
taken with the permission of
Eileen and Ed Takayesu

## INTERNET RESOURCES

*www.town.east-hampton.ny.us*
Town of East Hampton official site.

*www.lauderhill-fl.gov*
Lauderhill, Florida, site of Herb
Sadkin's Leisurama south.
*www.worldsfairphotos.com*
Bill Cotter's photo collection.

*www.pxarchive.de*
Montauk Link Archive Project, for those
who want to believe.

*www.fortunecity.com/marina/sea
farer/665/index.html*
Camp Hero and Montauk Air Force Station Website which includes a virtual tour
of Fort Hero.

## A NOTE ON THE FIGURES

To preserve a sense of visual flow, a
number of figures appear out of sequence
and/or are not referred to in the text.
This is purposeful but will still drive any
editor reading this nuts.

## LEISURAMA
## A DOCUMENTARY FILM

If you haven't already seen it on PBS,
Jake Gorst's documentary *Leisurama* will
be available on DVD soon.

Visit *www.leisurama.info* for more
information.

For more information on Leisurama visit
the Montauk Library on the Montauk
Highway (Route 27), just east of town.
You can try asking at the Montauk
Chamber of Commerce. But expect some
funny looks.

## COLOPHON

The body text of this book is set in DTL
Documenta, a serif typeface designed
by Frank E. Blokland in 1990. The balance
of the type is set in Futura, a sans-serif
designed by Paul Renner in 1927; and
Monterey, designed in 1958 by Intertype.

Published by
Princeton Architectural Press
37 East Seventh Street
New York, New York 10003
For a free catalog of books, call
1.800.722.6657.
Visit our web site at
www.papress.com.

© 2008 Princeton Architectural Press
All rights reserved
Printed and bound in China
11 10 09 08  4 3 2 1  First edition
No part of this book may be used or
reproduced in any manner without
written permission from the publisher,
except in the context of reviews.

Every reasonable attempt has been
made to identify owners of copyright.
Errors or omissions will be corrected
in subsequent editions.

Editor: Jennifer Thompson
Designer: Office of Paul Sahre with
Peter Ahlberg

Special thanks to: Nettie Aljian, Sara
Bader, Dorothy Ball, Nicola Bednarek,
Janet Behning, Becca Casbon, Penny
(Yuen Pik) Chu, Russell Fernandez,
Pete Fitzpatrick, Wendy Fuller, Jan Haux,
Clare Jacobson, Aileen Kwun, Nancy
Eklund Later, Linda Lee, Laurie Manfra,
Katharine Myers, Lauren Nelson Packard,
Arnoud Verhaeghe, Paul Wagner, Joseph
Weston, and Deb Wood of Princeton
Architectural Press
—Kevin C. Lippert, publisher

Library of Congress Cataloging-in-
Publication Data

Sahre, Paul.
  Leisurama now : the beach house for
everyone (1964–)/Paul Sahre.
    p. cm.
  Includes bibliographical references and
index.
  ISBN 978-1-56898-709-5 (alk. paper)
  1. Seaside architecture—New York
(State)—Montauk—History—20th cen-
tury. 2. Housing—New York (State)—
Montauk—History—20th century. 3.
Montauk (N.Y.)—Buildings, structures,
etc. I. Title.
  NA7575.S24 2008
  728.7'20974725—dc22

                        2007042486